The Make It Happen Man

The MAKE IT HAPPEN MAN

10 WAYS TO TURN OBSTACLES INTO STEPPING

STONES WITHOUT BREAKING A SWEAT

BOB PROCTOR
LIFE
SUCCESS
PUBLISHING

DEAN STORER

LIFESUCCESS PUBLISHING, LLC
8900 E. Pinnacle Peak Road, Suite D240
Scottsdale, AZ 85255

Telephone:	800.473.7134
Fax:	480.661.1014
E-mail:	admin@lifesuccesspublishing.com
ISBN:	978-1-59930-045-0
Cover :	LifeSuccess Publishing. LLC
Layout:	Lloyd Arbour & LifeSuccess Publishing. LLC

COMPANIES, ORGANIZATIONS, INSTITUTIONS, AND INDUSTRY   PUBLICATIONS: Quantity discounts are available on bulk purchases of this book for reselling, educational purposes, subscription incentives, gifts, sponsorship, or fundraising. Special books or book excerpts can also be created to fit specific needs, such as private labeling with your logo on the cover and a message from a VIP printed inside. For more information, please contact our Special Sales Department at LifeSuccess Publishing, LLC.

Printed in Canada

TABLE OF CONTENTS

ACKNOWLEDGMENTS

I owe my deepest gratitude to...

My wife, Janet, for her phenomenal love, trust, and friendship while allowing me to follow my dream, and for her unwavering support through the whole process.

My daughter, Heather, for her ongoing help with the book and for her creative abilities in bringing the stories to life.

My daughter, Heidi, for her willingness to listen and help in any way necessary and for giving support with her positive attitude.

The team at LifeSuccess Publishing for coming together to help make my dreams a reality while keeping my vision always at heart.

Every obstacle that ever arose in my life for making me the person I am.

DEDICATION

To my mother and father for all the accomplishments and failures they experienced in life. They taught me to make my own choices. My parents may not have always understood me, but they did their best to support me and for that I am grateful.

ENDORSEMENTS

Dean Storer has changed my life in many ways. From the very first time we met, Dean has been a positive influence on my family and me. I now have hope for the future. In addition, I have seen many incredible changes in my life. Due to Dean's coaching, we now have healthier bodies, a positive mind set, a closer family relationship, and a brighter financial outlook. Because of the opportunities that have been presented to me, I now have a purpose, vision, and a friend. I am very fortunate to be associated with him.

– Larry Braun and Family, LifeSuccess Consultant

Dean Storer brings his life experiences full circle. This is evident in his teaching and his infectious positive attitude that has brought awareness to new heights in my life, providing a definite shift in my everyday experiences. Thank you, Dean.

– Penny Davis, Owner of Zen Bella Spa and Salon

I met Dean about two years ago. During that time our relationship has evolved from an acquaintance, a very positive one, to an extraordinary friendship. He has been a very affirming mentor whether he or I realized it at the time. He believed in me when I didn't believe in myself, and he continues to support my thoughts and ideas.

Another common phrase Dean says is, "Just make the decision." I attended The Science of Getting Rich seminar in August, which was huge for me. That was one of the decisions Dean encouraged me to make. The cost to attend the seminar was miniscule compared to what I have learned and use in my life. Dean was on fire after the seminar, and after the training in Florida, he set up three Master Mind groups in central Oregon. I had the privilege to be in the first group, and we graduated in November. I am currently facilitating a group in my home.

   – **Gail Ottlinger,** Nikken Wellness Consultant

Reality is a question of perspective; the further you get from the past, the more concrete and plausible it seems — but as you approach the present, it inevitably seems incredible.

   – **Salman Rushdie**

FOREWORD

By Jack Canfield
Co-Creator of the Chicken Soup for the Soul series

I have written many books with the desire to help people realize their dreams and watch them come true. *Chicken Soup for the Soul, The Aladdin Factor* and *The success Principles* are just some of the books I have written to aid people on their own journey and it gives me great pleasure to watch people like Dean accomplish their dreams and help others like he is doing with this book.

The Make it Happen Man helps pull you from your view of hopelessness and put the spring back in your step and the sparkle back in your life.

By Bob Proctor
Bestselling author of *You Were Born Rich*

How we view the world and react to our circumstances determines how successful we are in our lives. Unfortunately, most people don't realize that we have the power to choose to make our lives better rather than just accepting what is. Dean Storer relates through personal experience that you can not only change your future for the better, but you can get past the events in your life that have slowed you down and kept you from exploring your true potential.

The Make It Happen Man is a book that attracted my attention immediately. It illustrates how you can create future success by changing your thoughts and actions right now, a principle I've been teaching for close to 40 years. It stems from the idea that you can tell what you have been thinking by looking at your results. While you may say you have positive goals and understand these life changing principles, if you are not experiencing success, then the problem lies not with your goals, but with your *thoughts*. The mind is an incredibly powerful tool, yet we rarely use this power to our advantage.

With more than 25 years of personal experience in counseling others and living these concepts, Dean uses practical examples to show how we sub-consciously internalize circumstances and situations, and how that continues to affect us for years without even realizing it. Instead, if we studied and increased our awareness, we would be in a position to choose the path we desire rather than merely accepting what life hands us.

This book is testament to Dean's caring nature for others and conveys the lessons he's learned through trial and error. *The Make It Happen Man* provides the stepping stones to lead you from the lackluster results you may be currently experiencing to the abundance you deserve.

I encourage you to read this wonderful book from cover to cover. It carries powerful information that will move you from autopilot to creating the life you really want.

INTRODUCTION

Life is a constant growing process and though the work is never complete, it does become easier, the lessons take less time to sink in, and you realize the journey is well worth achieving your desired outcome.

While working on the content for this book, I saw a mock up for the cover that said, "Forwards by Bob Proctor and Jack Canfield." Though it was only a sample, I immediately committed to turning those words into reality. I went to the LifeSuccess Consultants training in Florida, which was led by Bob Proctor and Paul Martinelli. After arriving, I spoke to Gerry Robert and stated that I wanted Bob to write my foreword. Gerry explained that Bob stopped doing forewords some time ago, but this answer was not something I was willing to accept as I had committed to having his forward in the book. I decided to ask Bob myself.

Toward the end of the seminar, Bob was in the back of the room preparing to leave. I saw this as my opportunity and approached him. Though my whole body was racked with nervous excitement, I looked him straight in the eye and asked if he would write the forward to my book. He paused, and then looked away. Finally, he said, "Okay."

Ecstatic and overjoyed, I thanked him and went back to the training with a spring in my step and a smile on my face. I had accomplished the first part of my goal. Now I just had to find a way to get in touch with Jack Canfield to make it complete.

I discovered that some of the teachers from *The Secret* were holding a seminar in Toronto, Canada, that I really wanted to attend so I decided to purchase the ticket. Unfortunately, when I went online the next day, they were sold out. I called Cheryl from Paul Martinelli's office to see if she knew how I could get a ticket, she also stated they were sold out and that they could not get a ticket for me either. Still, I held the image of attending the seminar in my mind and right after I got off the phone, she received an email stating that a woman had some tickets available. Cheryl called me within minutes. I got the ticket and prepared myself not only to get Jack Canfield to do my forward, but to also gain knowledge from these wonderful people that had become teachers of *The Secret*.

As I got off the plane, I tried to imagine various ways to present my request to Jack Canfield. Jack is a talented and successful man, and I wanted to make sure I presented myself accordingly. I watched as everyone else from the plane received their luggage, but mine never arrived. I had an attendant check, and found that the airline had lost my luggage. I was wearing traveling clothes and all my business attire was in that luggage. I felt myself getting upset thinking of the things I needed for the next day's seminar, which I now would not have. It didn't take long for me to realize lost luggage was not something I had control over, so I changed my attitude and went about getting the essentials I would need.

The next day I awoke, showered, and put on the clothes I had traveled in the day before because I still did not have my suitcase. I arrived at the seminar with another 2,000 people. As I seated myself, I wondered how I would ever get Jack's attention with this crowd. Feeling a little grungy because I was wearing yesterday's clothes, I left to stretch my legs at the break. As I came around a corner, there stood Jack Canfield. I called out his name and asked if he had a moment. Though late for an interview, he stopped. I quickly told him I was writing a book and that I would like him to do the foreword. I handed him a flyer I happened to have in my pocket explaining what I do. He looked at me and said, "No."

I was a little disappointed, but I had been visualizing Jack's foreword in my book for more than six months and I was not taking no for an answer. I went back into the seminar and listened with an open mind and an open heart. The announcer stated that Jack Canfield would be downstairs signing his book at lunch, and I thought this would be a perfect opportunity to speak to him again. However, when I went downstairs, he was gone. Jack spoke to the seminar attendees after lunch, and I was moved by his talent and accomplishments. This made me more determined than ever to get him to write my foreword.

On the last break of the day, I ran into a friend of mine from the LifeSuccess Consultants seminar in Florida and we began chatting. When I looked up, I saw Jack about 10 yards away. I yelled out his name and walked over to ask if he had any time. He told me no, but I was determined so I said I would be grateful and honored if he would join Bob Proctor in writing a foreword in my book. He told me Bob was enough and turned to leave. I gave it one last shot and said, "Jack, in your speech today you said most people don't get the things in life they want because they don't ask. I'm asking." He turned, looked at me, and said, "Okay, I'll do your forward."

I was engulfed in a throng of people walking all around me as I stood stunned. It finally hit me that he said yes. A huge grin spread across my face. I said, "Thank you!" As I watched Jack leave for his appointment, I was elated and amazed. I created a goal in my mind and completed what I set out to do — against all odds and in spite of so many people telling me it would never happen.

As I look back on the past obstacles I've encountered throughout my life, I've now learned to view them in a new way. The many lessons we go through are not wrong turns; they are part of the journey. My own road has had many twists and turns, and all of my past experiences make me who I am. If any of those circumstances were changed or taken away, I would be a different person than I am today. This isn't to say that my life has been filled with only pleasant and wonderful relationships and events. That's not true of me, and it's probably not true of you, either. Each difficulty we overcome makes us stronger – but only if we let it.

"The Law of Attraction attracts to you everything you need, according to the nature of your thoughts. Your environment and financial condition are the perfect reflection of your habitual thinking."

– Joseph Murphy

Through our own thoughts, we literally attract and create the physical reflection of what is being held within our minds. Positive people are usually surrounded by others who think and act in the same positive way. You can feel this positive energy when you're around them. Conversely, negative people seem to attract crowds of other negative people, and they never get out of the hole they are in or understand that they don't have to remain in that negative pattern. There are choices available to us all. We can leave negativity behind and develop positive thoughts and actions. One follows the other.

Anything that you can imagine is within your reach. If you can think it, you can create it. Everything you do and have is a product of what started as a thought or desire in your mind.

The Law of Attraction is considered a fundamental universal law that applies to everyone. It is very powerful once you understand how this law works and learn how to tap into it for yourself. The Law of Attraction works somewhat like a magnet. There is energy and vibration in everything on this earth and in the universe, and that includes people. You can use it consciously and with purpose, but it is at work in your life whether you choose to use it or not. You will get whatever you focus on, good or bad.

In the following chapters, you will see that the steps to using the Law of Attraction in your life include clarifying what you want, learning to focus on that goal, and seeing its achievement in your mind. There is vibration in your thoughts, which is why we feel comfortable participating in certain activities or being around certain people. We are attracted to those with a similar vibration and this becomes our comfort zone.

Once you are clear about what you want, focus on it, and see it in your mind, then you must take action and step out of your comfort zone. You will attract people and things that will help you achieve your goals. Maintain positive energy and feel good about it.

As great things and positive people are attracted into your life, you must accept them and continue on your way. Sometimes it's difficult to keep your thoughts doubt-free and act as if you have already achieved your goal. Think and talk about your dreams in the present tense, and avoid words like "maybe" and "someday." You should also know that there is great power in being grateful for your dreams even before you get what you want.

". . . brothers, whatever is true, whatever is noble, whatever is right, whatever is pure, whatever is lovely, whatever is admirable – if anything is excellent or praiseworthy – think about such things."

– The Apostle Paul, Philippians 4:8

If you are wondering if it is possible to turn obstacles into stepping stones without breaking a sweat, the answer is: YES! The question you must ask yourself is, "Who put the obstacles there in the first place?" When you focus on your obstacles or problems, that's all you see. A wise man once said that where your focus goes, your energy flows. If you think about obstacles, you get more obstacles. We fight and resist the stumbling blocks in our way. My grandpa called this process "Making mountains out of mole hills." What we don't see is that all the energy spent fighting and resisting just gives us more roadblocks to overcome.

We must look beyond these obstacles with the creative side of ourselves and see the landscape of possibility and success. That is when we see the stepping stones that lead to solutions instead of the boulders that prevent us from making progress. This process starts with you, but don't think that you must accomplish these things all by yourself. If you try to make life a test of individual endurance and strength, you will wear yourself down and stop moving forward from sheer exhaustion. When you work with others as a team, the load becomes much lighter and the possibilities endless.

As you put the principles presented in this book to work in your life, there are three basic concepts that will help:

• Look beyond the problem to the solution – this is key to forward motion.

• At each stepping stone, stop to enjoy the journey with eyes of compassion and a grateful heart.

• Let go and let God.

CHAPTER 1
AWARENESS

---

*"I therefore claim to show, not how men think in myths,
but how myths operate in men's minds without their being
aware of the fact."*

– *The Raw and the Cooked*, 1964. Overture

Most of us go through life on automatic, not really aware of where
we're going or where we have been. Then, we wonder how we could have
gotten where we are. Woody Allen once said, "Half of life is just showing up."

How you and I practice our awareness can create a prison or a
sense of freedom. It is totally up to us. Daily life hands you the book on
experience, and you must walk through it to gain the lesson. Your actions are
dominated by trial and error instead of intention.

When we do things absentmindedly, we do them unconsciously.
We just drift from one experience to another, ignoring most of what goes on
around us unless we feel threatened.

Then we react in one of two ways: We either run away or defend ourselves, generating what psychologists call a "flight-or-fight response." Many of us think we are victims of everything that happens to us. When we just don't bother to pay attention, we miss things that are right in front of us.

You can have a better life if you operate consciously and with intention. It begins with being aware of yourself and of what's around you. Practicing awareness builds understanding and the ability to recognize things. If we think about ourselves and our bodies, most of us go around every day oblivious to what is going on inside of them. Thus, awareness is the beginning of the path to becoming enlightened and living a better life.

We're going to start with the basics and then work outward from there. The first step to becoming aware is to *stop what you are doing - right now.* Spend a few minutes in silence. Turn off the radio, turn off the television, stop talking, and listen to your surroundings. I want you to experience each of the five senses completely. Don't hurry through this section just to get through the book faster, or you'll miss some of the gems I have to share with you. Take your time. You need to really experience each one of the senses available to you — seeing, hearing, smelling, touching, and tasting. They are each so familiar to us that we don't even think about them anymore. The only time we pay attention to one of them is when we experience something very bad or really good.

I find that if you take the time to be aware of every little thing for this exercise, you will build a stepping stone that can help you find the real you – the internal you. It may seem a little elementary, but we have to start with small things to build the path. When playing a board game, your token begins on "Start" and then you go from there. This is our starting place for the part of the journey we're taking together.

If you are inside, look around and notice – the color of the room, how many windows there are, what the furniture looks like, and then continue in this manner until you consider all those things you see with your eyes. When you've taken in everything and consciously named it to yourself, turn around and look at the rest of the room. If you make quarter turns, stop and observe each section of the room until you've made a full circle, so that you don't miss anything. Be sure to notice even the smallest items, like a pencil on the table. How many books are on the shelf? What are their titles? Study the pictures in the room one at a time, and notice every detail. If you're finished with this first sense — seeing — in 5 or 10 minutes, look some more. You've probably missed things that you walk past everyday that don't even register anymore.

Relax into actually seeing what is around you. Don't let your eyes flit from one thing to another until you have consciously made a note of what it is. If other thoughts pop into your mind as you look around, try to recognize that you had that thought and let it go. Don't let your mind wander if something reminds you of a chore you forgot to do. If there is dust on the electronics in your entertainment center, now is not the time to think about when the last time was you stopped to really clean this room, and now is not the time to clean it up. Everything you see is part of your surroundings. That's all. You can clean later if you want to.

Next time you are riding in a car on a busy street you travel all the time, look around at signs, buildings, new construction, or other things you hadn't noticed. If you are the driver, you need to pay attention to the road and not the scenery, but you can still notice things.

Have you ever played games where you look for a list of things in a picture? It sharpens your eyes and the way you look at things. Think about it. The more you consciously use your senses, the more aware of them you are. Doctors say that when someone loses one of their senses, the others become more active to make up for what has been lost. If you can't hear, you have to be able to see in order to read lips or see sign language or read.

If you are outside, you need to treat where you are like a room and observe everything around you in quadrants, just like you did inside. Be sure to observe everything within your range of sight. You are probably in your backyard, but if you are in a larger area like a mall or park then limit yourself to a specific area. I'll bet you'll see things you forgot were there. At home, you may even find something you lost.

The second sense I want you to enhance your awareness of is hearing. First, close your eyes to shut off any visual hints. Just rely on your ears. Sit quietly for about 15 minutes. What do you hear around you? Are there voices coming from another room or from outside? Concentrate on what sounds appear to be made inside the room where you are. If you are outside in your backyard, limit your conscious efforts to only those things inside that area. I want you to temporarily think of yourself in a box. Identify every sound.

At first, you may not hear much of anything, but just sit silently and wait. Don't keep opening your eyes to see how much time has gone by or you won't get a full awareness of your sense of hearing. You could set the alarm on your watch or cell phone to go off in 15 minutes. Don't respond to people talking around you unless it is an emergency. Answering the door or the telephone is an interruption in your experience.

In a few minutes, you will realize there are many sounds. The wind in the trees, the dog's paws padding across the floor, a car passing with a loud radio, children laughing, the hose dripping against the stepping stone by the house. Can you hear yourself breathing? It will surprise you how many sounds there are that you consciously tune out or ignore.

Remember what it was like when you were growing up and you slept out in the backyard or went camping? Everyone went to bed. It was dark. And you heard every sound for a 10 mile radius and tried to identify it, even the unknown. That is the kind of concentration I want you to experience.

Next, what can you smell? You can keep your eyes open or closed for this part of the exercise in awareness. Are there flowers? Is someone cooking, and do you smell the fragrance of charbroiled steaks wafting through the air? Is there an unpleasant smell in the wind? Can you smell approaching rain? Does the kitty box need changing? The baby?

Sometimes a certain smell can trigger a memory of someone you care about or an episode from your past. The freshly mowed lawn may bring back memories of playing in the grass cuttings as a child, or sweating as a teenager when your father made you mow the lawn on hot summer afternoons. For this experience, I just want you to identify the things you can smell.

You could do this as you drive down the road and pass restaurants, fields of flowers, the park after it rains, or maybe a feed lot or an oil refinery. Everything and everyone has a scent of some kind. If you have a girlfriend, you probably recognize her perfume. Your boyfriend or husband may wear a certain after-shave that you know when you smell it.

Think about your favorite fragrances. Imagine what they really smell like. What is your favorite food? You could even go to a department store and smell the perfumes and men's colognes. Do certain stores have a unique smell to them? Let your mind and your senses experience it together.

Briefly think about how your behavior is affected by different smells. Scents can make you hungry, excited, or calm. You may want to get away from one and feel attracted by another.

The fourth sense is feeling, or touching. Blind people see with their fingers. I'm sure everyone has seen the advertisement on television where a young blind guy is at a party with his girlfriend. He leaves to go to the bathroom, and when he comes back, he says to her that she needs to see the bathroom.

Think of how sensitive your fingertips are when you have to go to the doctor and have a blood sample taken. It hurts for a couple of days.

Walk around the room where you are touching things. Not briefly, but take time to touch them and rub your fingers back and forth. What are the textures that you feel? Consider the carpet, the furniture, drapes, and tabletops. In your yard, touch leaves, grass, chairs, tree bark, or the dog. If you need to, close your eyes and concentrate on the experience. (But if you have a dog, be careful where you touch the grass.)

There is a game that children play. They put different kinds of things in a paper bag. Nobody can look in, but when it is their turn they have to put their hand in and guess what it is by how it feels. Think about all the different ways those things can feel. Some are smooth. Others are grainy, like sand. Still others will be wet, dry, rough, soft, hard, flexible, rigid, gooey, and so on.

Fur is soft, but when you touch different kinds you notice they have different textures. A rabbit fur is soft, but a German Shepherd's coat is bristly.

If you had some coats hanging up, could you figure out which one was yours in the dark? Leather usually feels soft, but it can be stiff. A wool coat may feel rough to your hands. Anything that is knit, like a sweater, is lumpy from the stitches.

We can also feel temperatures. Hot and cold are different sensations, but we can also experience ice as hot if we can't see it. We can tell if something is liquid or solid. Think about the different textures of the food we eat. All of these things make up our sense of feeling or touch.

For the next one, you may need to go into the kitchen if you're at home. If you're outside, you could put leaves or produce from plants in your mouth. However, I warn you to be extremely careful of what you put into your mouth. *Do not* put anything in your mouth that you don't know is safe to be eaten or swallowed. Taste fresh herbs or suck the honey from the honeysuckle bush in your yard. If you have a garden, taste the fresh vegetables. Think about the difference between fresh-off-the-vine tomatoes and the ones at the grocery stores in February.

You could treat this like one of those tasting parties. Have you ever been to a winery where, after the tour, you got to taste all the wines they make? You taste one. Then they give you a piece of plain French bread or a cracker between wines to clear the other taste out of your mouth, then you taste another one.

Think of how much fun it is to go to Sam's Club or Costco on a Saturday to shop. They almost always have food samples for you to try. It is an experience for your sense of taste. Each thing either appeals to you or it doesn't. You might buy it, or may never want to eat it again. We all have our favorite things we like to eat or drink. It is a result of how we are affected by the little taste buds on our tongues.

Look in your refrigerator or go to the store and look at all the options you have to choose from. You will see bottled water, soft drinks, milk, juices, even your favorite beer.

Let yourself treat each taste like a new experience. Enjoy each bite of what you eat. Remember the first time you had ice cream? Have fun with building your awareness of tasting.

I want you to go one step further in discovering your physical senses. Stand in a safe place where you won't hit anything if you lose your balance. Close your eyes. Wave your left hand around in the air. Pay attention to what the air feels like, and be aware of where your hand is moving. Now, repeat the same motion with your right hand. Open your eyes and sit down. While this exercise does not demonstrate one of the five senses discussed, it is called proprioception, or the awareness of your body's position. It is the sense that we use to know where we are and where the parts of our body are. It is in our unconscious self.

Most of us spend our lives merely experiencing sight, sound, smell, touch, and taste with little conscious awareness. We have little concept of proprioception. We are adrift. Our focus on the physical realm never allows for the development of our spiritual side. While we are learning about this "sixth" sense, let's look at the Law of Vibration. It is a part of the overall Law of Attraction, but in some ways it is like proprioception. We are probably not aware of it.

Scientists tell us that everything in the universe vibrates. A simple explanation is to think about what happens when you drop a pebble into water. You can see little rings flow out from where the stone went in. The little rings spread out until there isn't anywhere else to spread. Bob Proctor explains it this way: "I am a soul, a spirit, non-physical, and I live in this physical body. And I have the ability to dictate the vibration that my mind and body will be in."

If you read about what things are made of, you will find that everything is made up of molecules. If you took a corner of one of the pages of this book and tore it off and put it under a powerful microscope, you would see something that looked like tiny particles moving. That is the vibration you aren't normally aware of. Everything that you can see, touch, smell, or hear is made of molecules that are in constant motion.

The vibration or movement that takes place inside the molecules, and then every thing the molecules are in, creates energy. Different things vibrate at a particular rate or frequency. Those things that vibrate at the same frequency will work together. I don't want to get too deeply into the physics of this phenomenon, but I do want to share with you the basics of how it works so you will be able to tap into both the Law of Attraction and the Law of Vibration. They work together. Becoming aware of them will help you stimulate and guide your power to create the things you want.

There is also a spiritual side to this Law of Vibration, but we will get into that side of it and how it affects us in a later chapter. Let's stop a minute and talk about our unconscious and conscious selves. That part of us that is the unconscious is unaware or suppressed, but some of our impulsive behavior comes from there.

We have a subconscious working in our brains that is only one step under our conscious thinking and actions. We can tap into our subconscious and use it as a tool in getting those things that we want out of life. Meditation is one way to tap into it to make a difference in our results. We will discuss this in more detail later in the chapter.

When we are conscious, we can feel, think and be aware of what's going on around us. That awareness includes our perceptions of what we see as our reality. It includes not only recognizing things, but also being alert and able to observe. Our thoughts, our emotions, and our five senses are all part of the process.

I've learned that each of us is comfortable inside our self-made prison, our "mental box of perception." The key to unlocking it lies within your reach. You need only take hold of it and let your spirit out. When the mental box of perception is opened, you are free to realize your creativity and your full potential as a human being. That inner power is a combination of both our *abilities* and our *possibilities*.

It took me years to understand, but I learned that if we are growing from our experiences then we will always be outside of our comfort zone. But we seem to prefer to stay within our self-imposed limits, which unfortunately can become what I call *The Misery Zone*. I became locked in my own misery and thought it could never change. I wanted to escape, but I lost my sense of self and tried unsuccessfully to bury the pain.

When I was 14, I went swimming in the Green River with two of my friends, Jim and Kevin. A bend in the river created a section of calm water and a beach, but we had to swim across some rapids to reach it. We stood on the bank with Kevin's dog, a German Shepherd, contemplating the rough water and fast-moving current. Jim and I were pretty strong swimmers, but Kevin wasn't. He thought he could swim 20 feet or so, but no farther. As we climbed down the rocks to the water's edge, we discussed a plan to get all of us across the river safely. The Green River at that point stretched about 20 feet across, as closely as we could figure.

Jim and I decided to swim across first and take the dog with us. After we got to the other side, Kevin would yell to let us know when he was going to jump in. We planned to help him get across the rapids if he needed any assistance.

Acting like typical 14 year old boys, we played on the beach as soon as we arrived, not looking back or paying attention to Kevin waiting on the other side. He must have become frustrated waiting, or we didn't hear him call to us. The next thing we knew, Kevin had jumped into the current with a splash. His eyes stayed closed and he slowly dog-paddled, trying to keep his head above water. He never made a sound, or at least we couldn't hear him over the sound of the rapids.

The current quickly took him downstream. Jim and I ran down the rocks along the shore to try and reach Kevin, but we realized he couldn't fight the pull of the rapids by himself. We jumped into the water and fought our way to him. Kevin bobbed up and down and looked like he was about to go under.

When we reached him, Jim tried to get a good hold on Kevin's torso. I dove under him and held his legs up. Seconds seemed like hours. Jim probably thought I had drowned. As I struggled to push Kevin up to the air, I realized my mouth was wide open and sucking in water, not air. My lungs ached. I knew I had to get to the surface if I wanted to go live. I had to let go of Kevin if I was to survive.

Jim struggled to keep his head above the torrent. Kevin slipped from his grasp. We struggled to some rocks and held on. We turned to look for Kevin. He had disappeared.

Further downstream a man was fishing. When he saw us struggling in the water, he ran to us and shouted, "Is everything okay?"

Over the roar, we yelled, "Call 911! Kevin's drowning!"

By the time the ambulance and police arrived, we knew that Kevin must have floated downstream some distance from where we lost him. We found Kevin about 300 feet past the rocks we had clung to. His body was under water. One of the officers ripped off his clothes, dove in wearing only his underwear, and brought Kevin to shore. As the officer laid Kevin's body down on the rocky sand, it became apparent that he had drowned. It was too late.

My low self-esteem already affected my behavior. By 14, I had already turned to experimenting with drugs and alcohol to get rid of my feelings of guilt, shame, and fault. The tragedy of losing my friend Kevin plunged me deeper into depression.

I thought I had failed Kevin and his family. I believed it was my fault he had drowned. Knowing that I was there when my friend needed me most and that I had been powerless to help him in spite of my efforts caused me to want to escape from the reality of my part in a failed rescue.

Over and over, I went through ways I thought I should have been able to save him. I felt totally responsible for his death. It seemed the only way for me to deal with the pain was to submerge myself deeper and deeper into drugs and alcohol. I wanted to forget everything. I needed the pictures in my mind to stop. It felt like punishment for my inability to change what happened. I hated living with these overwhelming feelings.

When I wasn't trying to bury my emotions through taking drugs or drinking, I expressed my rage by fighting. I chose to fight whenever any complication came into my life. I took the tragedy of losing Kevin and made it worse. The issue became larger and larger. I compounded it by taking an exaggerated responsibility for the incident. I was unaware that I had a choice to take this experience and use it to make my life a cherished gift.

I locked myself in the *Misery Zone* by concentrating on only those things I could see, hear, smell, feel, or taste. I needed to find clarity in my life and tap into the inner self, the spiritual part of me. All too often we ignore the development of our spiritual side. We don't realize that it opens windows and brings clarity to our minds. It is where our creativity comes from, and it represents who and what we truly are.

You're probably asking, "Just what do you mean by 'clarity,' Dean?" The dictionary defines clarity as a "state of being free from ambiguity or indistinctness," and a quality of being lucid, plain, or evident. To possess clarity means we are able to perceive clearly, as in a clear intellect or a clear head. Our thoughts are unclouded.

As I tapped into my inner self, I became more discriminating. I was less clouded with passion. I reacted less with my emotions and more with my mind. It later manifested itself in me over time with a serenity I had not known before. I experienced more positive feelings and more positive circumstances.

We all have painful experiences that represent out darkest times. If we could, we would erase them. I know I wanted to change what happened to Kevin. I didn't know at the time that my life's experiences would mold me into the person I would later become. I just wanted the pain to go away. Whether things are good or bad, taking them completely away would be a mistake. Our character is built through them all.

"If you will call your troubles 'experiences,' and remember that every experience develops some latent force within you, you will grow vigorous and happy, however adverse your circumstances may seem to be."

– John Haywood

Now, go back to the experience of your senses. We started with physical awareness through your five senses. Then, we moved on to how your proprioception worked. You knew in your subconscious where your body was, and where your hands were when you waved them in the air. Maybe for the first time you have intentionally experienced bringing a feeling and knowledge from your subconscious into your consciousness. That is part of your inner self, your spirit. It's available to you if you learn how to tap into it. We will go into more depth about spirit in a later chapter.

Your awareness of yourself and your surroundings doesn't achieve anything by itself. Basic knowledge without growth and action gets you nowhere. However, if you stumble along the path of life, learn from each experience, and apply it to the next obstacle; there is progress to be made.

"What lies behind us and what lies before us are tiny matters compared to what lies within us."

– Ralph Waldo Emerson

I mentioned meditation earlier in the chapter, and now I want to share some things I've learned about using it in my own life. Some people see it as just being still or praying. But it's both more and less than these things. The fact is that meditation can be a valuable tool in becoming aware of yourself and the abundance around you.

People in the past have often thought of meditation as a peculiar ritual of Eastern religions and not something that Westerners would use.

However, it is becoming more accepted than it used to be. True meditation is a discipline in which you turn your thoughts inward and concentrate on a particular object or awareness. Some people use it for personal development; that is what we are talking about here. It will help you focus and be more aware of all that you are, inside and out.

Meditation is a practical tool for tapping into your deepest thoughts. It helps to clarify things. Some people use it as a stress reliever or quiet time alone, but it is more than that if you use it right. You can use it as a form of prayer, but prayer is more an active process of communication with God or who you see as a higher being. Meditating is focused on you and your personal growth and development. That's what we are trying to work on together in this book.

People who meditate everyday often find they are clearer about things and more focused when they are working or involved in activities. They feel calmer and more joyful. They are more at peace with themselves because they are getting to know themselves better. It actually creates more positive energy, and that in turn will attract positive experiences back to you. Try meditation as part of your path to awareness.

The first steps of becoming aware are a conscious act. The following Personal Coaching Activity will begin this process, but remember that by itself, it doesn't get you very far.

PERSONAL COACHING ACTIVITY

We are going to begin this coaching session with some personal reflection. Be honest with yourself. Only be aware of these beliefs on your list. Try to state them without emotion or attachment. Treat each one as only information. The KEY to this exercise is to REMEMBER that this is ONLY to help you become more aware of your beliefs as a basis for change.

1. Make a list of beliefs you hold about yourself.

2. Go back over the list. Think about where those beliefs may have come from, and make a note reflecting the source next to each item on your list.

CHAPTER 2
BREATHE

"There is the fear that we shan't prove worthy in the eyes of someone who knows us at least as well as we know ourselves. That is the fear of God. And there is the fear of Man — fear that men won't understand us and we shall be cut off from them."

– Robert Frost

Have you ever noticed that the first thing we do when we are scared is to hold our breath? From childhood to adulthood, it is the same thing. The dictionary calls breathing the animating force within living beings. We have to physically inhale and exhale, or we will die. But breathing is more than that. Some primitive cultures believed that your breath was literally your spirit. They believed that the spirits or souls caused life in people, just like our breath does. The soul was a vapor. With no written language, primitive people couldn't explain it any other way.

For our purposes, life is a process much like breathing. When we are frightened, our feelings can easily move to a sense of helplessness. We are convinced that we are at someone's or something's mercy. Next, we sink into hopelessness. Fear can take only an instant to travel this path. It pulls us like quicksand to a place we cannot escape. Or can we?

Keep breathing. The "monster problem" facing you may not be as large as it first appears. When you're afraid, you experience physical symptoms like the catch in your breath, the twist in your stomach, and adrenaline shooting through your body.

"The great problems of life are always related to the primordial images of the collective unconscious. These images are really balancing or compensating factors which correspond with the problems life presents in actuality."

– Carl Gustav Jung

When you are breathing normally, it is an unconscious activity controlled by your brain. If you stop and think about your breathing, you can consciously control it. But normally it goes on as a function of life that we take for granted. Just as you can voluntarily hold your breath or force it out of your lungs, you don't have to remain in the quicksand of your fears.

Until we learn to let go of our fears, it is hard to make changes in our behavior and our experiences. Nobody can go back and change the things that have happened in the past. But we must, always start from where we are now. If we change our thoughts and actions, we make a different ending than the one we might have come to. We have to create the change in ourselves, or we let our circumstances become the guide for our behavior.

Within 12 months after losing my friend Kevin in the Green River, I had developed a habit of running from my problems. If I wasn't physically running, drugs or booze supplied my escape. My refusal to face any conflict or problem was my decision. When I fought with my girlfriend or experienced difficulties at home, I left. School represented numerous obstacles that I didn't want to deal with. I avoided them at any cost, not realizing that I was paying the biggest price.

For years, I didn't know my bad attitude was making my life worse. It only added to my problems. Now I realize that I caused a lot of the fighting myself. I didn't notice how much it impacting my life.

Thoughts about Kevin and my past mistakes and failures overwhelmed me. If I ever came up for air, I was consumed with grief, regrets, and felt so depressed that I had to dive back in to escape. I set myself up for a future of repeating my past, but I didn't know it at the time.

The summer I turned 15, I left home for parts unknown. I didn't care where. I just wanted to be anywhere but where I was. With a sleeping bag and a change of clothes, I hit the road to hitchhike around the country. At first, I felt an exhilarating sense of freedom. There was no one to tell me what to do. No one to call me stupid. No one to fight. However, before long, an emotion I hadn't expected set in and clouded my days and nights-loneliness. It wasn't that I hadn't felt lonely before, but this was different. I was isolated from everyone and everything I knew. I didn't want to be home, but the isolation became really hard to deal with.

Then, fear set in. I couldn't run far enough to get away from it. I think I held my breath each time a car stopped to give me a ride. With each ride, it intensified. Never knowing who might pick me up was a new experience that grew into periodic panic. What if no one picked me up and I was a hundred miles from anything? What if some nut gave me a ride and I never got out of the car alive? What if someone ran over me in the dark as I stood by the side of the road?

One day, while waiting for a ride at the top of the pass going into eastern Washington, a car stopped to give me a ride. I'd been standing there for a long time, but I felt a little strange about this guy. Because I needed a ride, I shoved my reservations away and climbed into the front seat. It didn't take long for me to realize that it was not a smart move.

As soon as I shut the car door, we took off. I couldn't smell the alcohol on his breath, but it wouldn't have made a difference to me. I soon realized that he had been drinking - a lot. He was plastered, and was weaving all over the road. I held my breath until my lungs begged for air, and then only took quick gasps. I sat, white-knuckled, hanging on to the armrest with one hand and the dashboard with the other.

I was so scared that I couldn't speak. I couldn't tell him to stop and let me out. If that part of the ride wasn't hair-raising enough, after coming down off the pass, we came to a crossroads with a four-lane highway. There was a stop sign for the cars on our route. The speed of the car never decreased. I jammed my feet against the floor and braced for the crash.

The car rocketed through the stop sign and across the four-lane highway intersection. Realizing all too late that he had run a stop sign, he slammed on the breaks. We skidded to a stop half way onto the shoulder and past the highway. By the grace of God, no one hit us, and the car didn't roll and kill us both.

I got up my nerve and found my voice, "I'm getting out here!" I remember standing on the side of the road as he stomped on the gas and careened off into the distance. I almost kissed the ground. This was my first trip away from home. Alone and afraid, I did not know what direction to go. Looking back on that experience, I see it as a picture of the way my life as a teenager had been.

I was like a ship with no sails and no rudder. I felt lost and adrift, with no direction or power. Like the waves beating on the sides of the ship, life kept beating on me. I wandered from place to place, relationship to relationship.

I thought if I ran far enough, took enough drugs, or drank myself senseless, the problem would disappear. But you can't outrun yourself. Steven Covey puts it this way, "No matter where you go, there you are." Don't expect to escape yourself. Sooner or later, we all have to turn and face the person in the mirror.

I made excuses and blamed the world. I never looked at myself. I always said I had problems because of the way I was brought up, or because my bad relationships made me miserable or angry. I blamed my friends or anyone else I could think of for the direction my life was going. I wouldn't take any responsibility for my problems. I was always saying that no one understood me.

There are many excuses people use to explain the failures of their lives. All they do in the end is trap themselves in the prison of their mind and thoughts. I realized years later that I was creating my world by my thoughts and the words I spoke.

You might be saying to yourself, "Just hold on a minute. What do you mean that my thoughts create my world?"

If you look at it again, you will notice that I said *I created* my world with the thoughts that I was thinking. The more I learned about the Law of Attraction and the role of positive thinking, the more I found freedom through the se concepts. I learned to take on a healthy responsibility for my own thoughts, actions, and circumstances.

I realized that if I hated someone and talked about them in a bad and slanderous way, I saw and felt the effects of that energy coming back to me and my life. Looking back on those years, I can see that when I was with my friends, and everybody started talking about fighting, the next thing I knew we were in a big fight.

I was so controlled by drugs back then that if we ran out of them, a fight always broke out. My dependency on alcohol was the same way. Becoming aware of my drug and alcohol problems was like coming around the corner to find one of the biggest, meanest, 800-pound gorillas standing before my eyes. I'd been blind to it for a long time.

Let's take a look at the real you while we travel this path together. It's not easy, and it's sometimes the last thing you want to do, but take the awareness of your breath and think of it as a divine spark. It is a force within you. Your spirit, or life force, is within you and can be tapped into. It's up to you to decide on a better way to handle the obstacles that hinder your progress in life. Like the construction workers who blast away the boulders and mountains, you can blast away monoliths you see in your path.

We need to keep breathing through it all. Remember that fear is just a state of mind. We get so busy being afraid that we don't accomplish anything or change anything. Most people don't know that we can realize success in our lives only one stepping stone past our biggest mistakes and failures.

Think about going to the movies. Some people love suspense or mystery, action or romantic comedy. Others like movies based on Stephen King's novels or scary movies that always have someone trapped in a house at night. Usually the electricity goes out, the phone line is cut, and the characters are at the mercy of some crazed person who wants to kill everybody - definitely not a "feel good" movie. What I want to draw from that is how you feel while you're watching it. You probably want all the lights on and want to sit close to someone you can trust not to grab you in the ribs at the scariest part. You can't take your eyes off the screen, but you're terrified to watch. You may have pulled your feet up off the floor and assumed a fetal position while still sitting up, if that's possible. You hold your breath. Even though you stopped chewing your nails years ago, you just started the old habit again.

By the time the movie is over, you are exhausted. Your adrenaline has pumped gallons through your body. At least with a movie, you know it isn't real; it's just a story that someone wrote and filmed for entertainment. Not all of us agree that it is entertaining, but we don't actually die from it, either.

Letting fears about your future get the best of you is like how watching a scary movie uses up your energy. It doesn't help you move forward or get you any closer to your goals. It becomes an obstacle that you think just won't go away. However, you can defeat it.

I've heard people ask the question: How do you eat an elephant? Answer: One bite at a time. When you face your problems one at a time, you begin one breath at a time. Piece by piece, the elephant becomes smaller and more manageable until it is completely gone. Each mouthful is a step on the way to success — the replacement of old negative feelings with positive thoughts. When you're finished with the first one, celebrate. Then tackle the next elephant.

We learn, and then take those lessons and incorporate them into our behavior and thoughts. We have the option to accept or act on the things we learned. When we change how we think and look at things, we change our circumstances and our actions, one by one.

In my reading of self-help and personal development books, I've also read about networking and network marketing. I think that some of those same principles can be applied to the steps I take to turn my dreams into realities. Over the years, fear is what has stopped me from doing things. Now I'm learning more and more how to work through those feelings. Zig Ziglar says, "Fear?... False Evidence Appearing Real." What a great way to put things into perspective.

For me, this statement is a reminder that my fears can be an emotional reaction to something that happened when I was in school as a child. The self-image problems I've faced so many times were based on untrue things that were said to me. Those feelings are part of the old "tapes" and beliefs I used to hold about myself. I'm not stupid, even though people told me I was and then treated me that way. As an adult, I now know I've probably had ADD most of my life. I may have done some stupid things, and maybe you have as well, but that doesn't make either one of us stupid.

ADD is a learning challenge diagnosed all the time now. Back when I was in elementary school, the testing process for learning disabilities wasn't as advanced as it is today. So if a child didn't fit the average mold of what everyone was supposed to be, teachers labeled them "stupid" or "slow." They put them into special education classes to help them learn, but there was a stigma attached to it. I got labeled for my actions, not for who I really was. After a while, my actions reflected that I felt stupid. I did things that only reinforced it. Then the next time I faced the same situation, I was afraid of what I was certain would happen.

Most of you probably watch one of the *Law and Order* television shows. In every episode, you can see the police detectives gather evidence and figure out who the killer is. We are like that when we look at our own behaviors.

I used to see myself as stupid, aggressive, and hard to get along with. I thought and acted that way. My thoughts became my actions. Whenever I had to face a problem at home, I ran away. (Sometimes from home, always from the problem.) Away from home, a disagreement with somebody usually ended in a fight. I blamed everyone else for my behavior. Looking back, I can see that the evidence proved to me that I was a troublemaker. I didn't understand what part I had in creating my experiences.

I reacted in a way I was sure I would. It was always negative. What I didn't understand was that I caused the evidence that I saw as proof. Therapists call it a "self-fulfilling prophecy." I was convinced that I would act a certain way, and even worked on my "tough-guy" attitude. On the inside, I didn't want to be that way and didn't know that I was the cause. I was the opposite of what I wanted to be because that's what I thought about.

The last two words of Zig Ziglar's concept are "appearing" and "real." What we see is not always what is really there. We have a natural filter in our brains that focuses on the direction that we always go. We see like a horse with blinders on. It's like those pictures you look at and see one thing, and then after staring at it until your focus changes, you see something entirely different. What appears to be true is not always true; it's just how we perceive it. That is how we create our own reality. We can only see it from our own viewpoint.

When I first started to help others as a minister and a life coach, it was scary to approach new people. As I gained confidence in myself and in my ability to help others through my own experiences. I didn't feel so afraid.

The more I stood in front of people giving sermons and speaking to groups, the more I found I wasn't afraid to do it anymore. I worked my way through it. I changed my way of thinking and was able to push past the old problems I'd hung onto for so long.

Likewise, the more I learned about the techniques of network marketing, the more I realized it was like anything else. I had to practice and apply it to my own experiences, and use what would get me where I wanted to go. It was another one of those positive tools I attracted into my life.

Sometimes, while we are standing around holding our breath, we think that when things aren't so scary that we can do what we really want to. If we wait for the perfect time, it will probably never happen. We are always going to be faced with obstacles. We just need to get started. With every step we take, we get stronger and closer to our goals. We learn the skills and tools we need to accomplish what we want and become more self-confident.

Personal Coaching Activity

You're going to make two lists. This may be difficult for you to do objectively. Try to step outside of your feelings and do this without negative energy. Look at the experience as if it is someone else's, if you can.

1. Make a list of four or five things that you see as your biggest problems.

2. Journal on another piece of paper what it is about these problems that makes you feel frightened or doubtful. What is it that blocks you from making this problem go away, that you have control over yourself? This is a healthy way to express your feelings and thoughts without attacking anyone else or blaming them for your choices. Be honest with yourself.

3. If you didn't have any of those stumbling blocks keeping you from changing that problem, what would the results look like? Brainstorm and journal possible solutions or steps to eat this elephant one bite at a time. Nothing is too far out to consider or too small to consider. Don't let yourself settle for, "If the problem was gone I wouldn't have to deal with it anymore and life would be better." Think of actions you can take.

By looking at what you believe to be obstacles, you are beginning to identify foundations for making them into stepping stones. Keep going. Every path starts with the first step, and every other step is progress.

CHAPTER

SELF-IMAGE

"A child's self-image is more like a scrapbook than a single snapshot. As the child matures, the number and variety of images in that scrapbook may be far more important than any individual picture pasted inside it."

– Lawrence Kutner

Our self-image is the basis for everything. You'll never outperform that image you hold of yourself. Everything you have seen or heard in your life becomes a part of that picture. Things we heard as a child were put into our subconscious. That programming became the way we saw ourselves and how we looked at the world. What you think about, you become.

For starters, our image is what we look like, our physical shape, how we did in school or sports, and what kind of value system we have adopted from our parents and family. What kind of relationships we have with parents, brothers and sisters, grandparents, extended family members, other children at school, and authority figures helps decide who we think we are.

If we have unfinished goals, or don't like the way things turn out, the feelings from those experiences help define how we think about ourselves.

Our image also affects our creative process. We look at ourselves through a pair of glasses that only sees what we've experienced in our past. For example, if you see a picture of a football game, a set of tapes begins to play in your mind. One might be the memory of the time you won the game in the last 10 seconds by receiving a pass from your best friend and running into the endzone for a touchdown. You were able to break a block, and throw yourself across the goal line as the game ended. Everyone cheered. Your coach pounded you on the back, and all the players crowded around you. Your father was so proud he popped the buttons off his new shirt bragging about your athletic abilities. You were the hero of the day.

Another view of the game might see you trip over the foot of the player blocking you. You fumble the ball as you go down, falling flat on the grass. The other team recovers the ball, and they run down the field to score the winning touchdown. Everyone on your team is mad at you. The coach yells at you for not paying attention, and your father tells you how clumsy you are in front of your friends.

How we see ourselves is an internal mechanism that tells us who we think we are and what we think we are. It is positive or negative, depending on our experiences and how we look at them. Sometimes the image we have of ourselves is rational, but sometimes it is irrational. Part of our image is tied to how we think other people see us, or what they think about us.

A mental tape you carry with you plays over and over each time you see a football game, or hear about your neighbor's son playing on the high school team. It becomes a part of how you see yourself: clumsy, disappointing, unable to finish what you start, unfocused. If you had been the hero of the game, your tape is completely different; you see yourself as innovative, strong, a quick thinker, irreplaceable. Each tape is very different, but each is just as powerful in creating your image.

We take those things that happen to us and internalize them. Our image of ourselves is a combination of all the things we've been labeled since childhood. I have lived with labels all my life: son, student, brother, husband, provider, protector, father, friend, landscaper, cook, baker, and a candlestick maker, just to name the good ones. Not one of these is who I truly am. These are just labels, and even though I have been these things, I am so much more. Self-image includes qualities and how we see our self-worth. Somehow we draw the conclusion that what is said to us is the reality of who we are. I thought because it was hard to learn, I was stupid. Because my father didn't spend any time with me, I felt like he didn't care about me. If my own father didn't want to be with me, why would anyone else? I thought I was unacceptable at home, and since I didn't fit in at school, I was unacceptable there, too.

The first time I remember feeling stupid was in grade school. I had difficulty reading and processing math. Sometimes it was difficult to understand the directions for a task. The school assigned me to a special education reading class. There were only three or four of us in the class because we had been set apart from all the other children. I felt totally different from every other child I knew. I was somehow less than everyone else.

Since my parents worked all the time in their own business, they were too busy to realize what was going on with me in school and how I felt about myself. Looking back at it now, I know I must have had some type of learning problem. No one stopped to test me to see if there was a reason for my inability to do well in school. I was being passed from one grade to the next, just to get me out of a system of education I didn't fit into.

One time in fifth grade physical education, I couldn't understand the instructions our teacher gave us about playing volleyball. Standing in the back of the gym in a line with the other children, I felt confused and didn't know what I was supposed to be doing. When I didn't perform the action the teacher wanted, he became angry and raised his voice. Still not understanding what he wanted, the teacher grew increasingly upset with me. Finally, he threw the volleyball so hard at me that I wet my pants in front of the entire class. I was embarrassed and humiliated. The other children laughed cruelly and made fun of me. The teacher was no better.

I couldn't take my problems at school to my parents and expect any help. They didn't understand me, and we fought over me getting into trouble at school. My own frustrations soon grew into anger. That same year, I started playing football as a way to release my built-up aggression. Sports were the one thing I really loved as a child.

Unfortunately, in junior high, I took a required speech class. Of course, each student was expected to give speeches in front of the class throughout the semester. Since I'd been labeled in grade school as stupid, it followed me into the new classes. By that time, I was convinced I was the label that others gave me. I was convinced I couldn't learn like the other students. No one told me that I wasn't the only one terrified to stand up and give a speech.

When the teacher called my name, I got up from my seat and walked to the front of the classroom. My fellow students were merciless with their taunting and laughing as I began my speech. Part way into my recitation, I was so embarrassed by their reaction that I ran out of the room. I sat through the rest of the semester in that class, but never did another speech. I took F's rather than go through that experience again.

Every incident like these at school reinforced my belief that I was stupid. I thought about it all the time. As a young boy, I didn't know that what you think about, you become. If I had any positive reinforcement while I was growing up, it couldn't compete with the negative things said to me. The negative feedback is what played over and over in my brain. I think I always wanted things to be different, but didn't know what to do about it or how to change it.

Going through puberty seemed to make my problems that much bigger. I didn't know that it's normal for boys to go through it at different rates. Some children mature up to six years before others do. As a teenager, all of us want to be in the middle of things and be part of the group. The hardest part is when it seems like you are always too tall, too short, too fat or skinny, too hairy or not hairy enough. Your skin is either too pale or all broken out with acne. You have a five o'clock shadow or nothing to shave yet. You never fit in. I didn't know that everybody else was going through some of the same feelings. I thought it was only me, and that made me angry with everyone because I felt different.

I've learned that my self-image is linked to my own expectations and the expectations of others. I saw myself as unimportant and stupid, a misfit, and so I acted that way. My brother was always smart and did well in school. It seemed easy for him. It was really hard for me, and my parents and teachers said things that made me think I was stupid. They acted disappointed. I became what I thought was expected of me. I was supposed to be a below-average performer at school, so I was. I pushed my hurt feelings down until I got angry. The only thing I excelled in was football, but I ultimately ruined that for myself by acting the way everyone expected me to — badly.

My self-talk agreed with the tapes that played in my brain. I ran myself down like everyone else did, and the more I did it, the more I believed it. I thought it was a picture of me that was true.

Since then, I've learned that we can each change our lives. We may not be able to change the past, but we can choose to make the future better. What we believe about ourselves drives where we are going.

"A belief is an agreement I make with myself that something is true."

– Paul Nakai

We don't realize that with each belief we hold about ourselves, our self-image comes from the agreement we hold ourselves to. That's why it is so difficult to change how we see ourselves in the mirror. We are resistant to realize our real potential. We get stuck in a place of feeling negatively about ourselves in every aspect. It's kind of an all-or-nothing way of thinking. If one thing is bad, then everything is bad.

Here is an example of how stubborn our negative beliefs about ourselves can be. There was once a man who was absolutely convinced he was dead. He saw all kinds of doctors and counselors, but no one could change this powerful belief he held. A psychiatrist agreed to see the man, but after several months, he got nowhere. Finally, the doctor told the man, "Okay, look. I want you to go home and for the next 30 days, once each morning and once each night, I want you to look at yourself in the mirror and say, 'Dead men don't bleed.' You got that?"

The man said he understood. Thirty days later, he was back. The psychiatrist asked him, "Did you do what I said?" The man said, "Yes, Doctor. Twice each day, once each morning and once at night, I looked at myself in the mirror and said, 'Dead men don't bleed.'"

The doctor said, "Fine. Give me your finger." He took the man's finger, pricked the tip with a pin, drew forth a drop of blood, and said, "There! What do you think of that?"

The man looked at his finger and said, "MY GOD! Dead men *DO* bleed!"

This is an example of how powerful our beliefs can be. Sometimes they are irrational like the man in the story. We don't have any real concrete evidence to support that belief, but we are sure it is true. Your self-image may be the product of something that happened to you as a toddler, something you don't even remember. It is locked up in your in your subconscious mind, and when it comes out into your active thoughts, it is expressed as behavior. In behaving according to these old tapes, we frequently do things that cause ourselves or others to validate the false belief. With a lifetime of reinforcement, we eventually turn into what these tapes describe. The good news is, *you can change the tape!*

Changing those deep-down entrenched beliefs is hard to do, but I found that over time, I really could change them. I could replace them with better, healthier, and more positive beliefs. I had to learn to use the filter in my conscious to stop certain thoughts. That way I didn't have to unlearn things that weren't true about me. I could work on positive thoughts and actions and build up positive beliefs and results.

When I was still running from my problems, I thought I could run fast enough and far enough to leave them behind. I knew I wanted my life to change. I tried doing it by myself, one thing at a time, no plan or purpose. But I always woke up each morning to the same person. Since I couldn't do it myself, I turned back to my old friends — drugs, alcohol, and fighting. Albert Einstein once said that the definition of insanity is doing the same thing over and over and expecting different results. If you repeat the same mistakes over and again, can you really expect a change in your lifestyle?

My experience tells me that when I repeat the same things that I've done before, the results will remain the same. No lifestyle change. No new tapes in my head to play. No positive experiences to replace the bad ones. We must be willing to break that agreement with ourselve, break whatever the beliefs are that hold us back. You keep yourself from becoming a better and happier person with a more abundant life.

"Science and psychology have isolated the one prime cause for success or failure in life. It is the hidden self-image you have of yourself."

– Bob Proctor

You're trapped and don't know that you have the ability to let yourself out. I didn't think there was a way out of my circumstances. I was wrong.

Scientists have learned through studying how our brain works that those things we spend more time on create strong neural connections in our brains. Those activities and thoughts we spend less time on have weak neural connections. If you make a concerted effort to think something positive, that thought generates a new neural pathway, becoming deeper and deeper the more you think about it. Unfortunately, the same holds true for negative thoughts. However, those negative thoughts or tapes you're listening to in your brain can be consciously stopped. Those once-strong impressions will become weaker and weaker until they almost disappear from lack of use.

I think the world has two kinds of people – positive and negative. Other people classify the two groups as optimists or pessimists. How we choose to use our past experiences and old tapes determines which group we are part of. If you are an optimist, you see problems as opportunities. Thus, they become something to find solutions for, not to stop you in your tracks. Obstacles may show you new possibilities if you don't get stuck in your negative mindset. On the other hand, if you are a pessimist, you always see the worst of any experience. You look for the worst and always find it. You just want it to go away, so you don't have to face it or solve it.

Problems are only possibilities that you haven't found an answer for yet. For me, I wanted to take the easy way out. What I didn't know was that if you always take the easy way out, you will never grow. You'll just stay the same as you are, and life won't get any better. Even if it doesn't get worse, you don't progress or grow. We bore ourselves with the same old thing going on in our lives day after day. Nothing looks promising. We don't change because we don't let ourselves. I hung onto the past and its negative energy partly because it was comfortable, but also because I didn't know what to do about it. I didn't know when I was young that tools were available to me to make the changes I really needed to make, so I could be the person I really wanted to be. I wanted to help other people get out of the same traps I experienced, but I had trouble at first keeping *myself* out of them.

When I started learning about setting goals as part of the path to help me out of the holes I kept digging for myself, I found that the way I reacted to the goals and how I set them made a big difference. If I chose an unrealistic goal or timeline, I would become frustrated with myself, because I fell short in the amount of time I thought it should take to get what I wanted. Then, frustration would start the old tapes and old behaviors. I also found out that if I tried to make my goals easy, I didn't feel satisfied or happy when I reached them. That didn't help me feel better about myself, either. Then, I came to the point where I realized that my goals could be challenging but still realistically reachable. It made me feel better about myself, and this way of looking at my goals was positive. It gave me a way to build up my self-image. It made me a stronger person.

One way to overcome your tapes is to start thinking about the qualities you have that other people don't. We each have natural skills, but we may not know what they are yet, or don't want to use them because of our past.

We are going to explore how to defeat those pits we fall into over and over. It won't happen all at once; it takes time to develop new habits and thought patterns. A new habit takes 21 days to develop. Sounds like a lot? Not really. Put it this way, in one year or 12 months, you will have created more than 12 new habits and pathways in your brain. It takes a conscious effort to stop an old tape and replace it with a positive statement, but you can learn to do it.

"The only limits in our lives are those we impose upon ourselves."

– Bob Proctor

Let's take a minute to look at pitfalls. They are kind of like potholes in the roads after a bad winter. You didn't see them the last time you looked or walked down that part of the road, but when you drive over them, the car bounces and upsets the passengers. That's kind of what pitfalls do. They can be dangerous and aren't easy to see ahead of time. You can't always avoid falling into one of them.

Sometimes they are a result of our own behavior. Many times, we set ourselves up for failure by not planning ahead. You don't have to think negatively to plan for handling problems. Just know that you can apply the lessons learned from your past experiences the next time you fall into a similar hole. It's a lot easier than coming up with a new way to solve the same old problem over and over. If the solution you have isn't working, you will want to find another. However, if the solution worked last time, then you should try it again.

So far, we have talked mostly about how people get a low self-image, and we've mentioned some ways to escape from the traps that poor self-image holds. I should also mention that professional counseling is a good option. If your self-image is so shattered, so wounded, or so depressing that you can't even feel like you might deserve something better. This book is not meant to take the place of counseling in any way. But most of us suffer from milder forms of low self-image. If you are in this group, then we — my mentors and I — have some ideas that might help you. I hope that by sharing some of my own story you will find the courage and determination to pursue a happier and more fulfilling life for yourself.

It's hard to build up your own self-esteem all by yourself. We usually can't erase the old tapes without help from others. When you think and act more positively, you will attract more positive and supportive people to you. You need to let others compliment and teach you, and then thank them for their help. Besides, it's a lot easier to walk a rough road with friends than it is to walk all by yourself.

I had to realize that other people thought I was worth spending time with and that they cared enough about me to nurture me. When we build relationships with others, we share friendship and love, and we grow closer to each other. It's okay for you to feel good about positive things and the people around you. After all, you deserve it. You may have to learn to repeat that to yourself several times a day to change a competing belief others have directed at you, but to feel like you deserve better is essential to actually having something better. Let me say this again: You deserve to have good things come to you in your life.

After talking to other people and reading about developing my own positive self-image, I found that affirmations were useful to the process. They can help you replace negative thoughts with positive ones by actively repeating them on a daily basis. Affirmations are just a statement of what you believe to be true. At first, you may not completely believe it, but if you open yourself up to possibilities, you focus on positive energy, and positive results that are in your future. Here's a tip, though: When using a positive affirmation, don't argue with yourself.

I found it works like autosuggestion. I listen to positive tapes and seminars, but these statements are personal for me. I take my intentions and turn them into a sentence or paragraph that describes how I see myself in the future, except it is said in the present.

I have learned that it works better if you create affirmations in the present tense, not the future tense. For example, instead of saying, "I will make a million dollars a year from now" I say, "I am creating a million-dollar income." Using these statements helps me to tap into my inner power and self-image in a positive way to produce what I want. We can actually reprogram ourselves using affirmations. They focus on the positive parts of our character. There are tons of affirmations that you can adopt for yourself in self-help books and on websites, but writing your own is a really good way to overcome your unique obstacles.

As I've already shared, we are what we say and think about. You can use affirmations for all the aspects of your life, the physical and the spiritual.

I also learned that I needed to accept myself and other people for who and what they are. We need to have a healthy respect for ourselves before we can respect each other; we must respect others to have them respect us. What I wanted for years was acceptance, but I went about it in the wrong way. I guess I figured that some attention for bad behavior was better than no attention. But before we can expect to accept others, we must start with ourselves. I believe that an early part of the process is accepting how we got where we are. We don't have to like or dislike it, but we must acknowledge it and, even more importantly, decide where to go from here.

Another thing I learned was to talk with other people about my experiences and my feelings. It's hard to do at first, because we may fear that other people will think we are stupid for making the mistakes we've made. This is rarely true, though. In most cases, everyone else has the same fear about sharing. But, if we don't share our experiences with each other, both the good and the bad, then we miss a big part of building a path to the better life we want. We learn from sharing our stories with each other.

Before we get started on the following exercises, there is one more lesson I want to share with you that helped me a lot. I found that other people who had been where I was and who had succeeded in changing their self-image had given me a model, a pattern to fit to my own circumstances. We can look at those we admire who are models of who we would like to be and then apply what we see in them to ourselves. We can do what they do to have what they have.

Before I started conducting seminars, I had attended quite a few as a participant. I was already used to talking in front of people by then, so doing seminars was a natural next step. I watched what they did, and listened to what they said and how they presented the material. I continued to study and read. I visualized myself doing what seminar facilitators do. I learned more skills and trained to become a real facilitator. I got past those old images of myself not being able to read or speak in front of people. I had learned that most people are afraid of speaking in front of a group of people. Through this process, I reworked my negative thoughts into positive ones, and that helped me push through my fear to become the person I was meant to be. It was one thought at a time, but we all start that same way.

PERSONAL COACHING ACTIVITY

Remember, each activity is a part of the process of changing your life into what you want it to be. Each step is important, just like each span in a bridge.

1. Make a list of the positive things about yourself. It is alright if it is a short list to begin with. Many people find it difficult to think of good things about themselves. We live in a world that criticizes more than it encourages. Get some help from a friend or family member if you need to.

2. Unfortunately, this next list will be easy for most people. Make a list of negative things you think about yourself. This is not meant to be a degrading exercise in which you beat yourself up. In fact, I want you to take the negative list and destroy it. DO NOT READ IT BEFORE YOU DESTROY IT!

3. Go back and read through your list of positive things about yourself. Write the first one on a 3" x 5" index card. Keep it with you all the time. Read it out loud in the morning when you get up and again in the evening before you go to sleep. Whenever you see the card during the day, read it to yourself. Your coworkers may not appreciate hearing your positive affirmations. If they ask you what you're doing, tell them you are changing your life – from the inside out. Repeat the routine for 21 days. Then, begin with the second positive and continue until you have gone through your entire list. Review the ones from previous weeks every few days to reinforce them. And remember, dead men DON'T bleed.

Congratulations! You've turned and faced your obstacles. It's a new beginning. You're developing the foundation for the first steps of a new life. We attract what we are and what we want.

THOUGHTS ARE THINGS
(Adapted from Henry Van Dyke)

I hold it true that thoughts are things

endowed with body...breath...and wings

and that we send them forth to fill

the world with good results...or ill

That which we call our secret thought

Speeds forth to Earth's remotest spot

Leaving blessings...or its woes

Like tracks behind it as it goes

We build our future...thought-by-thought

For good or ill...and know it not

Yet so the Universe was wrought

Thought is another name for Fate

Choose then thy Destiny and wait

For Love brings Love and Hate brings Hate

CHAPTER
DREAM

"Dream is not a revelation. If a dream affords the dreamer some light on himself, it is not the person with closed eyes who makes the discovery, but the person with open eyes lucid enough to fit thoughts together."

– Michel Leiris

I believe that each one of us is born with dreams inside us, and that we are here to discover and experience those dreams. Why is it that when we grow up we forget how to dream? Because we've been programmed to think that dreams are for children and you must give them up to grow up. In school, we are told to stop daydreaming and pay attention. They tell us to look at reality and get our heads out of the clouds. Dreams don't pay the bills. Dreaming won't get you anywhere. Do you remember hearing such things when at home or in school when you were a child?

It is not true!

While people around us are telling us that our dreams are unrealistic, think about it. A dream creates a picture in your mind. That picture is the beginning of what could be realized. If you can see it in your mind, you can make it happen. That's how inventors start out. Every invention that humans have developed throughout all of history started in this very same way. The process has a track record.

The dictionary says that to dream something up is to use your ingenuity in making, developing, or achieving what you want. So it goes from thought, to visualization in your mind, to a reality. Not letting other people discourage you from imagining a better life is the first step in making it come true.

We waste most of our time in a daily routine that someone else predetermined for us (*their* dream, incidentally), so we feel that we have no direction. Our lack of purpose makes us wonder why we are here. Some of us are able to hold onto our dreams through every experience, positive or negative, but others just give up. You don't have to let go of your dreams. You certainly don't have to surrender your own in favor of someone else's.

According to the Law of Attraction, you are already bringing people, things, and jobs into your life. Once you're aware of it, you can tap into it and attract positive things. You may be thinking, "Okay, Dean, am I supposed to think positive and sit around waiting, or is there more to it than that? I've heard all this before, but I'm not sure about how it really works."

Let's look at the process you can use. First, have a clear picture of exactly what you want. I have many dreams. One is to have a cabin in the woods, with a lake out back. There is a dock with a nice fishing boat. I can go hiking anytime I want. I also would like to own a brand new Harley-Davidson motorcycle. I love to travel, experience new things, and challenge myself. I enjoy starting new projects and seeing them through to completion. Each one of these dreams has a very real picture to go with it. I see myself at the cabin doing all the things I want to do there. I see myself on my new Harley with my wife behind me, riding down the Pacific Coast Highway on my way to California. This picture motivates me to create it in real life.

Next, focus your thoughts on your dream. You will attract people with like dreams to you, and you can help each other make them a reality. Remember, it is the nature of thoughts be expressed, and the form of expression is always an action. Then, you need to allow yourself to accept your dream. It's okay. It's legitimate. You can want whatever you want. Don't let yourself get stuck in thought patterns from the past when you thought you didn't deserve good things to happen to you. You do - never forget that.

When you're really focused on your dream, you get excited and build up positive energy and emotions. That creates a kind of vibration that attracts other things with the same vibrations. It's a little like changing the station on the radio. When the frequency matches up with the numbers you decided on, you get the music you could initially hear in your head before you actually heard it. You are literally on the same wavelength. When you're excited, you spread that enthusiasm to others, and they feel your emotions. You send out positive energy and get the same in return. Have you ever heard a speaker that just motivated you to the point where you wanted to run out and succeed right that minute? (In my dream, you're thinking of me as the speaker!) That's the feeling I'm talking about.

When it feels good, then take action with clear intention. Even though the universe will be in charge of "when and where," you have to take an active part in the process by committing yourself to the "what." While you're focusing, you will attract both what you need and who you need to succeed.

"Keep your dreams alive. Understand to achieve anything requires faith and belief in yourself, vision, hard work, determination, and dedication. Remember all things are possible for those who believe."

– Gail Devers

I kept my dream for 26 years. I wanted to help other people. Now I am, and I have been for several years through my past ministry and most recently through life-coaching and seminars. Discovering your dream creates a passion to see it fulfilled. That's what moves you forward to your purpose. Like uncovering a hot, burning desire, it shows you even more of your purpose – why you are on this planet.

Therefore, you have permission to dream. Allow yourself to. Don't limit it to small incidental things that you want or need. Get out of the box you've created for yourself. Turn it over, stand on it, and look at the view. Everything is within your reach. Remember when you were a small child and had to drag a stool into the kitchen to see the countertop where all the good things to eat were, just out of your reach? Remember how amazing it felt the first time you saw that wealth available to you and within your grasp? Feel that again.

Whether you call God or a superior being, your Creator put you here to experience a purpose and to fulfill it. This entity planted a seed for those dreams inside of you. Now it's time to water that seed and let it grow. Bring it into the light of day and let the light shine.

If you dream small, you experience limitations that you have put on yourself. If you dream big, the sky is the limit. Your dreams don't all have to be material things like a new car, a mansion on the hill, or a private yacht in the marina, but they could be. They could also be things like helping the homeless find jobs, or creating shelters for the abused and neglected. If you're thinking you would like to make $30,000 or $70,000 next year, why limit yourself? Dream big! Imagine yourself with a six-figure income this year and a million the next.

"If you dream it, you can achieve it. You will get all you want in life if you help enough other people get what they want."

– Zig Ziglar

Think about it. If all you want is a car that runs, that's all you'll ever have because that's all you ever talk about or look for. Instead, visualize climbing into that brand new, just out of the showroom car, and driving it away. See yourself wave to the salesperson, as you take your dream car off the lot and leave your old car behind. It all starts with becoming aware of the possibilities that exist and allowing yourself to dream in Technicolor. It's not magic! The dream and the thought need to become action. You will attract other people and opportunities to you in order to accomplish your goals.

When you have an idea about who you want to be or what you want to do, you make the idea the main thing in your life. You think it, dream it, and live it. It is your focus in your body and your actions, as well as your dominant thought. Concentrate on that dream and leave other things alone. I found out that is the way some people become great successes and spiritual giants in their fields.

We are responsible for what we become. Our dreams can become reality. We have the God-given power within us to remake ourselves. If we have made ourselves what we are through our desires, dreams, attitudes, and actions, then we can change our future by focusing on a new and better dream and life. I learned I could change my circumstances through a new mindset and actions that came from that change.

While working at the lumberyard in Arizona, I became a Christian. I found myself going to church more often. With the help of others, I quit doing drugs and alcohol. My purpose became clearer to me. I realized I could use my personal experiences to help others like me get out of the same situations. I soon realized I had a passion to help others, and that grew into a plan to become a minister.

However, my biggest stumbling block was the same old thing from school — difficulty reading and understanding what I read. This time I didn't give into the old tapes telling me I couldn't do it. I dove in head first. I started reading the Bible and became frustrated with my old problems, but I would not give up my dream. I knew there must be a way for me to teach myself to read and to become a minister. Many times along the way, I wanted to quit and return to my old "comfortable" lifestyle. That box I had built for myself was familiar and it felt good to me. It was tempting. But I had a desire to change and would do what I needed to reach my goal. I went out and bought a three volume set of Bible comic books. I could look at the pictures and read the captions underneath. It really helped me to understand the message. Driven by my passion to overcome the obstacle that reading had always been, I kept pushing myself to read more. I found that the more I read, the better reader I became. I taught myself to read. It was exciting, and I couldn't get enough.

Then, I slowly started reading more difficult books. Each step raised my reading level. I wanted to share my newfound joy of reading and the new worlds I was beginning to understand with everyone. My brother Jim lived in Arizona with me, and I wanted to read out loud to him. At first, the books were simplistic and I read slowly. He had always been good in school and excelled in reading, writing, and spelling, all of which I struggled through. He grew frustrated with me because he couldn't understand what I was reading to him as I tried to sound out new words. As soon as that frustration appeared, my old program from childhood ran in my brain. I immediately got defensive and wanted to quit. I wanted to escape. The same obstacle rose again to taunt me, but this time I learned to fight it off. My determination to succeed won out.My new journey was not an easy one, but I realized the life I had led was dark and depressing. I had a deep desire to help other people and continued to push myself forward. I chose to go through the long and tedious process of educating myself.

After three years of hard work and perseverance, I became a minister. My dream of helping others in situations like my own had been the core thought that kept me going. Preparing sermons was still a challenge, but one I enjoyed. I spent hours in the basement with my Bible, a highlighter, and a dictionary. Repeated reading of the scriptures gave me clarity. Looking up every word that I didn't understand brought me deeper understanding of my new faith.

One of the tools I developed for myself was a book of words. I wrote down any word I came across in my reading that I didn't know. Sometimes it felt like I was a child again.

In my private life, I had married my girlfriend and become the father of two little girls, Heather and Heidi. Still struggling to grow into a full adult myself, I was forced to learn how to balance being the head of my own household and a minister to others. Wearing the hats of husband, father, man, student, and professional felt overwhelming at times. I did not want to raise my daughters to make the same mistakes I had made.

"Learning without thinking is labor lost; thinking without learning is dangerous."

– Chinese proverb

My passion continues to be to help others. Each one of us has a dream and a passion that leads to our fulfillment. When you find something that interests you, explore it. Find out everything you can about the subject. Talk to others, read books, watch documentaries, visit the library, and ask the reference librarian to help you. Do a Google search on the Internet. Don't limit yourself to just one source of information.

After learning about your subject, how do you know if it's your passion? One way is to ask yourself what you think about when you first wake up in the morning and before you go to sleep at night. What would you rather be doing with your time than what you're doing now? Let yourself get emotional about it. What do you like to talk about? Whom do you want to spend your time? What do you make time for? These questions can help you find out what your burning desires are.

If you explore something and find you're not as interested as you first thought you were, that's okay. Everything you learned gives you more depth. You will be surprised at how that knowledge will come in handy. Enjoy the journey. Pick out another interest. Spend time learning about the new one, just like you did the last one. If your passion is working with children, then volunteer in an organization that gives you that experience. It may surprise you. Let the creativity inside express itself. Remember, your thoughts give you direction.

"All you need to do is think a certain way, move into action, think positively, see yourself already having it, move it into action, and attract it into your life."

– Bob Proctor

Another way to figure out what your dream or passion is to consider what would make your life better. Again, we start with you, but expand from there. Draw the circle larger and include what you want for your family and what you want to do to give them a better life. Keep enlarging the circle. What do you want to do to make things better for the people on your block, in your neighborhood, your town, your state, your country, and the world?

After exploring your interests and your passions, it's important to look at your natural strengths. Your dreams aren't limited, but if you have no knowledge or experience in medical science, you probably aren't going to be a lab researcher trying find a cure for AIDS next week. It is a noble cause, and you may support it in your feelings and may even donate money to finding the cure. However, you need to start at the bottom and be trained for the task if you really want to find the cure yourself.

Your dreams are the ones that come from deep inside and won't go away. One of the biggest obstacles we face is the fear that we can't do it. If we have a history of other people telling us that we are failures and that we never finish anything, then we have put that in our beliefs. It will trip us all the time.

Some people are actually more afraid of succeeding at their goal than they are of failing. They can think, "What if I do reach my dream? What if I become a nationally known – heck, an internationally known – speaker? Then what?" It scares them to think about the responsibility to all those people. Then they doubt their path and wonder why anyone wants to listen to them. It is possible to make our success a stumbling block by our doubts and fears.

Go back to visualizing yourself doing well at your dream. See yourself being ready for the daily tasks and knowing the information well enough to share it. Trust your experiences and the lessons you've learned. Most people will find something in what you say that is the same as their past.

A life full of disappointments and loss can make you depressed and feel like giving up. This obstacle can stop you in your tracks, but it doesn't have to be permanent. You can work your way out of it one small step at a time. That rebuilds your confidence.

When your obstacles to achieving your dreams seem to be too big to push through, sit down and breathe. Take a walk in the fresh air to clear your head. Relax in a hot bath for an hour, and leave all your worries outside the bathroom door. If you need to work through parts of your past with a professional counselor, then include that in your path.

It takes spiritual and emotional strength to dream and to make it happen. One thing that can help you is to visualize what things look like in your life on the other side of the obstacle. If you can't see around it, then use the visualizing tool. Remember, if you can see it in your mind, then you can make it come true.

Your actions need to be the product of clear intention. Be positive, and the things that you need will come to you in the form of a class or a book or a person. Often, what comes to you and helps you along your path is completely unexpected. You know you will attract what is needed, but you may not be sure exactly what that is. It's like putting together a 1,000 piece puzzle. You get down to the last 10 or 20 pieces, but some of the last pieces don't seem to fit like you thought they would. You know they have to go somewhere, but aren't sure where. All the things you need to finish are within your reach. A friend with a different perspective can sit down and helps you see what to do to complete the picture.It's sad to think about, but most people will die without ever realizing their dreams. I don't want to do that, and I'm sure you don't, either. You have it within you to dream and make it come true.

Focus on what moves you forward to reach your goal. If you are emotionally involved in making a better life for others as well as yourself, it has a bigger payoff than if you just focus on yourself alone. We're here to make a difference. That's why I hung on to my dream of helping others for so many years when I wasn't even sure how to help myself.

If you're not moving forward, you're probably moving backwards. What is the price of standing still or going backwards to you? It may be more than moving forward to reach your dream. You may suffer financially or in your relationships with your family. Such setbacks can affect your self-esteem.

The universe has a natural flow to the things that happen. It's like going to the Oregon coast and watching the waves come up onto the beach or the tides go in and out everyday. There is also a natural flow of things in your life. It comes from your thoughts and actions. What you think gives off negative or positive energy. You can push away those things that you want, or you can attract them to you. It is your choice. We determine how things will progress.

We also need to understand that the world doesn't work on luck. You may see one of your neighbors doing well at work and getting job opportunities and raises. They go out and put a pool in the backyard, purchase a summer condo with a great view on the coast, and buy new cars for themselves. Don't let yourself be driven by what you see others doing and accomplishing. You will focus on "lack" instead of your own dreams. If you are motivated by what others are doing and saying to make their dreams come true, you're probably giving up your own power. Focusing on someone else's world places you under their control instead of being in control over your own world and what happens in it.

Sometimes we give ourselves a timetable that we think everything should be done by. If it doesn't happen that way, we think we've failed. But you haven't because you're still moving toward your dream. We need to be a part of the energy flowing in us and in the universe around us. The universe and its timing are usually better than our own and are much more fulfilling. It gives us all what we need. Under our own efforts, we may be missing things along the way.

Deadlines aren't a bad thing, but they need to be realistic.

Look at successful people around you or in the news. They all had an idea that became a dream. One such successful person in 20th - century history is Charles Lindbergh. He used dream and his unrelenting focus to make history and create opportunities for millions of Americans. When Lindbergh was flying the U.S. mail in the 1920s, he knew that other fliers were thinking about the Orteig Prize of $25,000 for the first person (or crew) to fly nonstop across the Atlantic Ocean. At that time, airplanes were only 20 years old and few people flew anywhere, certainly not across the Atlantic Ocean. To travel to Europe, people did the sensible thing and took a ship.

Lindbergh wanted to be the person to make that first flight across the Atlantic. It became his dream and focus. He had a special plane built, the Spirit of St. Louis, and decided to fly alone. People told him it couldn't be done, but he did everything he could to move things forward until he could accomplish it.

On May 20, 1927, Lindbergh left Roosevelt Field in New York and headed northeast across the Atlantic Ocean. Thirty-three-and-a-half hours later, he landed in Paris. He made his dream come true. He believed in himself and accomplished what he set out to do. It began with a thought, grew to be a dream, ultimately became a passion, and finally became a reality. This shows us that anything we are really passionate about can be created.

After Lindbergh made that flight, the United States military caught on to the idea of faster transatlantic travel, an innovation that served this country well in World War II. Now, commercial airlines routinely transport several hundred people over the Atlantic Ocean in a matter of hours. If Lindbergh hadn't followed his dream, whose name might we be celebrating instead?

There are many, many stories about people who have dreamed and then brought that dream to fruition. Ford wanted to make an automobile so affordable that everyone in the country could have one. The first Model T was produced in 1908 and sold for $825. Now, most people have two cars in their garage. Steve Jobs and Steve Wozniak started Apple Computer in a garage in 1976.

Bob Proctor, Zig Ziglar, Steven Covey, and Robert Kiyosaki started with a dream of who they could be and what they could do to help other people make better lives for themselves. Now, they have built an empire. You can model yourself after those people you admire. It worked for them and it can work for you.

We have talked about facing obstacles and how we create them, however, we have to be realistic and know that they will happen. Don't be stopped by obstacles! Some people plan for them and how to handle them when they come up. Being prepared for things is okay as long as you don't keep focusing on the negative side of possible problems. You have faced and pushed through roadblocks before. Have the confidence that you can do it again.

PERSONAL COACHING ACTIVITY

Read through the positive list from the last chapter's coaching activity. Are you still repeating the thoughts from your index cards daily? Don't be discouraged if you miss a day. Just go back to it the next day. Keep going. Missing once, or even a few times, happens to all of us. The point is to pick up where you left off and continue until you have completed 21 days. Mark it on your calendar and celebrate. Now, let's take the next step.

1. Not sure what your passion is? Make a list of those things that interest you.

2. Reread your list. Put a number by each one in the order of its importance to you.

3. What are the top three? Write each one down on a 3" x 5" index card. Carry a copy in your wallet or purse, put one on the refrigerator, and learn everything you can about each, as we discussed in the chapter.

It will take some time to go through this process of finding your passion if you're not sure what it is yet. The great thing about the process is that you are building another stepping stone. You will find clarity, direction, and the hidden person within you. Push those negative thoughts away by repeating the positive ones you've developed in our activities.

CHAPTER 5
SPIRIT

"We are spiritual beings here for physical experiences, not physical beings here for spiritual experiences."

– Teihard de Chardin

The moment I tapped into my "spiritual side" I found myself more open and creative. My purpose became stronger. We are a package of mind, body, and spirit. The actual "you" is the spiritual part.

When we were children, most of us played games of "pretend." Boys liked to be G.I. Joe or a superhero. We imitated our favorite baseball or football players. We acted out what we saw on television or in movies. Girls often liked to be teachers, nurses, doctors, astronauts, mothers, or movie stars. They regularly looked up to cheerleaders and singers. But, at the end of the day, when it was time to take a bath and go to bed, we gave up our "pretend" games until the next day. What if you didn't have to forget your thoughts about who you are and the things you do and have? What if you got to keep that focus? Well, you can. Your thoughts aren't make-believe anymore. Your spirit is real, and the power and energy of your spirit can create a better life.

As adults, most of us wander through life never knowing that the physical body only represents part of us. We allow our body to become a box to protect us from everyone, including ourselves.

Will the real YOU please stand up? Come on take a chance. Let yourself out. It is one of the primary steps in realizing your full potential. Some psychologists put it in the terms of living in a garden. You have a choice to open the gate and let others in, or go outside the garden and experience everything you can only see from inside the yard.

One of the feelings we encounter is that of somehow falling short. We don't think we live up to the expectations of others. Satisfying parents can be a terrible burden on a growing child's shoulders. Everything you have observed or lived through is filtered through your own perception. Your perception is your reality.

If other people have put expectations on you that are unrealistic, like an 8-year-old working full-time and going to school, of course you can't do it. You're too young. Your body is still growing, and you need more sleep and time to play. You need a balance in your life so that you will grow to your full potential. You need to grow physically, but you need to be sure and let your spirit develop and grow. If you haven't used it, you'll need to learn how.

Some people are born pleasers. They never want to fail a parent or disappoint them. They become frustrated because they never seem to measure up. That becomes their belief and plays as another prerecorded tape in their brain. It can be devastating to a child as well as an adult.

For me, it seemed like I could never please my father. When I joined a church in Arizona, I transferred that belief about myself to my new relationship with a Heavenly Father. I figured pleasing God was out of the question. What I learned over time was that I had a spiritual side of me I could tap into, and this spiritual essence is who I truly am. Later, I realized the reason I thought I couldn't please my earthly father or my Heavenly Father was because I didn't take responsibilities for my own actions. The real person I could not please was myself.

"The state of your life is nothing more than a reflection of your state of mind."

– Wayne Dyer

Those first steps toward taking a healthy responsibility for myself and my actions were difficult and a little frightening. Actually facing yourself for the first time can be painful. I had to admit that everything in my experience up until then was a reflection of how I looked at myself – my self-image. In turn, it colored the way I viewed the world and the people in it. It was frightening to take responsibility for the negative and positive parts of me.

I'd spent most of my life seeing the world and the people in it as the problem. Nothing was my fault, or so I thought. Wayne Dyer says, "If that's the case, you're gonna have to send the whole world to a psychologist for you to get better." I had to admit my biggest problems came from within.

The more aware I became of my spiritual being, the more I began working on my true self. I raised my level of awareness and understanding of the freedom it released. My perceptions changed my reality. Once I understood the idea of being spiritual, not just physical, the world was mine for the experiencing. It was exhilarating.

Finding my true spiritual self gave birth to purpose in my life, and allowed me to be more creative than ever. The more positively I thought and acted, the more positive things happened in my life. When I slipped back into old habits of negative thinking, I learned to catch myself. I knew from the past that it would attract exactly what I didn't want. If I focused on the positive things, I felt reassured the result would be something I did want to attract.

Too many times we settle for whatever we get instead of attracting what we want. Low expectations and a frame of mind that comes from lack will end in lack. A high expectation followed with action attracts those things to you that you want or need. You can live in abundance. Bodies are confining; spirits are not.

Remember that no one has control over your thoughts but you. A choice is always open to focus on your dream and making it a reality. As you do this, you will attract others of a like mind. You can exchange thoughts and lessons learned from past experiences. You can help each other. None of us can do it all by ourselves. We need others, and they need us. Thoughts come from your mind, while feelings come from your heart. These combine to bring positive circumstances and opportunities your way. We forget we live in an abundant universe.

---

*"The greatest discovery of my generation is
that a human being can alter his life by
altering his attitude and mind."*

– William James

Let's stop and look at how our mind and spirit are linked. If we're going to use our spirit and its power to create a better life for ourselves and those we love, we need to understand a little about it. When we only focus on what we can see and touch, we are stuck like a car in the mud on a country road. There is an abundance of energy and potential in us that we don't realize we have. How can we recognize it?

To begin with, our mind has a conscious and subconscious part. We've talked some about it, but I want to go a little further because our subconscious is tied to our spirit. We have a choice to use our subconscious or not. We will still experience life, but it won't be in the same way. It's like seeing the previews for a movie, but never seeing the whole thing. You just get a little bit of what could be.

The information we take in from childhood by those around us and authority figures give us basic tapes of who we think we are and can be. In our conscious mind, we gather all those things in, and then it is fed to our subconscious mind. That part of us accepts anything that comes into it. So we take in either good stuff or garbage, and that weighs down our spirits. We don't use them. Then, the subconscious mind becomes the source of our images, feelings, and actions. The only way we can express things from our mind comes out in actions that reflect those deep images and feelings. If the input is negative, then we attract negative people and experiences.

Thoughts always motivate our actions toward what we want or toward what we don't want. The results are inconsistent if we don't have direction. We only experience a lack of opportunities because that is the only option. We have to change that from the inside — from our minds and spirits.

I know, you're thinking just how do I accomplish that? If it's hard to be aware and in control my subconscious, this isn't going anywhere. Well, I'm here to tell you that you can control it. It takes effort, energy, and persistence. You can use that power within you. First, you must make an effort to intentionally stop accepting negative feedback from other people. I'm not saying to ignore constructive criticism. I'm talking about pure negativity from some of the people around you. Reject it consciously. Only take in positive words and actions. Visualize the negative words as raindrops being shed by an umbrella or raincoat. They may hit the outside protection, but they slide right off.

Then, when you get positive words or actions directed at you, accept them with your conscious mind and feed them to your subconscious mind. It will accept what you send inside. You've changed what you're feeding your spirit. Like a seed, it will grow and break out of the shell into a healthy and gorgeous, productive plant. You will become a healthy, gorgeous, and productive person.

Remember that your thoughts are formulated. They are the tools of your spirit. They mold you as a person into everything that you could be. You govern yourself with the power of your consciousness. All your thoughts, feelings, and desires become beliefs. It also develops your personality, the part that others notice. Your potential grows because it is set free with your spiritual awareness. You will be energized by the process and will attract what you want and those to help you get it.

You probably never thought you could use the energy and power of your spirit to have a more abundant life. You can tap into it. However, don't force things. Let it happen. It takes a little time to learn how to bring about the daily use of your inner power. While you're practicing, you have the energy, and it will help you attract like energy in positive ways.

If you've never realized you had access to your spiritual inner power, it will be quite an experience for you. I know it was for me when I first learned about my spiritual power, and it has been a great ride ever since. It gets better and better the further along I am on my path to abundance.

Remember in the first chapter, when we talked about becoming aware of your physical surroundings as a first step to awareness of your spiritual being? We covered the five senses, plus one, proprioception. I learned from Bob Proctor that we also have six senses that link with our spiritual development. These are as valuable to use as the natural senses are. If you didn't have a sense of touch (feeling), you would pick up a hot object and suffer severe burns. In the same way, these factors will assist you in your spiritual life.

The first factor is perception, which is sensitivity and insight about the world around you. It is closely related to the proprioception that we discussed, but it also has a spiritual side. Everything we think, do, and have has a divine side.

The second factor is our will. We make choices and persevere when we use our will. In a spiritual sense, it is much more than that. It's not forceful, but focused. I found that the more I developed this skill, the better I could concentrate.

Memory, the third factor, is available to each of us. We have control over what we want to remember. It's amazing how our brains work! Just think, each thought and memory can be seen by scientists because of the creases and folds in our physical brains. We don't use it to its fullest capacity. However, we can have perfect memory. It is possible.

The forth factor, intuition, can pick up vibrations from others. It links with the Laws of Attraction and Vibration bringing like things into your life. People talk about "women's intuition", but everyone of us can use our gut feelings.

The fifth factor is your imagination. Continue to use and exercise your mind's eye. It is part of the process of visualization that becomes your reality. Think about it. Use your creative imagination. Not one person on this planet is without it. You just may need to get yours out and exercise it. Like muscles, a workout will build it up and make it stronger.

Reason is the sixth factor. It's interesting how we think things out on a daily basis, but never really use our power of reasoning. That ability is a tool you don't want to be without.

Make it a goal to tap into these six factors along with the awareness of your physical senses. When I discovered I have access to 12 senses, not just the five we learned about in elementary school, I realized I really do have what it takes to be everything that I want to be and to have everything I want. Abundance was in reach, and I could have it. So can you.

After you become better at attracting abundance through your inner power, you won't accept negative words or people, because they aren't a part of your reality anymore. The attraction becomes natural and easy, like breathing. When we are feeling good about ourselves, we have positive energy and vibrations.

Another thing that helps tap into our spiritual self is to get rid of old issues that we hold on to. Those will drag you down and take away your energy. I got rid of some of mine through counseling and others through taking responsibility for my own thoughts and actions. I had to learn to focus on myself and love myself, then on how I treated other people. As I changed myself, other things changed around me in more positive ways.

I also had to confront my demons when I gave up drugs and alcohol. They were of my own making, but I had to let those old beliefs go in order to free myself and let my inner self grow.

I finally had to learn to accept things about myself, my past, and what my future could be if I wanted to make the changes. I could be a powerful and joyful person using my spiritual power.

"Human beings, by changing the inner attitude of their minds, can change the outer aspect of their lives."

– William James

It is important to spend more of your time and effort on encouraging the flow of positive thought and feelings than on trying not to get into a negative mindset. You can learn to be your own monitor to be sure you don't fall into old thought patterns and behaviors simply because you are behaving on "autopilot" and aren't paying attention to yourself.

When we are surrounded by supportive people, we can help each other stay in a positive flow of thoughts. It is done in a loving and helpful way, not to criticize each other, but to encourage one another. We develop our inner power through our subconscious and conscious.

Tapping into your spirit is a learned skill that may take you some time to get used to. It is not something we are taught when we are children by the average parent. My parents were too busy working in the bakery to be enlightened. They were stuck in the rut of limitations they set for themselves. One thing my father did teach me was that you would never make much money if you worked for someone else. I learned that from him, but he wasn't aware of the other powers within himself he could have tapped into.

I am still challenged with using my inner power to its fullest extent. I've come a long way since I first learned about it. I'm not trying to say I have it completely mastered; it is an on-going process in my life. I just want you to be able to make your lives better. If I can help you through my experiences in learning about this spirit, the "true you," we will all be better off and live more abundantly.

Before we move on, let's take a detailed look at spirituality so that we can understand it better. We've already said that it is the inner you, the real you. What is it besides that? I found that the clearer my understanding is, the better I can use the tools given me to create my life.

For starters, I believe that our spirit does not have a limited amount of time. It goes on forever. It is a little part of the spirit of our Creator. The same power that was used to create the entire universe has a spark in us. We can tap that kind of power to make good thoughts and a better world. We have a connection through our spirit back to the Creator.

In this book, we are dealing with the spiritual side of us to be the inner power that we use to create what we want. It is centered on an inward focus to help us develop ourselves and grow past the obstacles in our path.

There are some key concepts that I am applying in my life and want to share with you. They can help us both on our path. Research by Martsolf and Mickley (1998) said that there are areas of spirituality that should be considered. The meaning of life is part of what we look for when we turn inside of us. It helps us find our purpose and make sense of our experiences. For me, the biggest part of that was finding that I created my life.

I learned more about being aware of my spirit being much bigger than I thought. It connects us with others and with a higher power. Thinking and learning about the potential of my inner self gave me a clearer picture of who I am and who I could become.

Some people in Western culture think that spirituality is linked with a religious belief and God. I found out that others think that religion comes from spirituality. For me, it is who I am.

When I tap into it, it becomes a powerful way for me to set goals that enable me to succeed in creating the life I want. Because it is never-ending, the inner me links up with will power and gives me a boost. I have found that it helps me get rid of the negative and untrue things that I thought. This is what helps us push past the obstacles we create. When the roadblocks appear so big to us that we can't get through, that's when you can go to your inner power and link to that energy.

Using our spirit and being aware of it can give us a more balanced life and contribute to our overall well-being. When things aren't working for you and it feels negative, you are attracting those experiences. I had to learn to let go and let my spiritual self out. Then I tap the never- ending positive energy of the creation, which is a natural part of the universe. The universe we see through a telescope is one huge creation. We are only one little part of it, but we vibrate like everything else does. We are part of it and we can have access to it. How powerful does that make you feel?

It makes me feel like there are no limits to what I can accomplish. I can do and be anything and create what I want.

Lots of people are skeptical about spirituality and how we can use it for creating a better life for ourselves and others. That's because we lock ourselves inside the same old box. They think that if you can't prove it's there, it can't exist. We'll get into more about how our beliefs affect us later.

"Strength does not come from physical capacity.
It comes from an indomitable will."

– Mahatma Gandhi

Gandhi is one of the people in history that I most admire. He was a spiritual man living in a real world. He was full of action, but not destructive. He didn't live a life filled with material wealth, yet he was a man who taught people all over the world because of his dedication to people. He was of service to others.

One of the reasons I admire him so much is that he is such a good example of helping others to overcome their limitations. It resonates with my dreams. I am not Gandhi, but we can all help each other. We can create better lives together with our friends and supporters.

Gandhi changed India forever and left an everlasting mark on the world. He was only one man, but he made an infinite impression. His spirit and ours are infinite.

He once said that it wasn't wealth that he wanted to change; it was the way that people used their wealth. If you enslave others with it, then it is harmful. If you use it as a blessing in your own life and share with others, it benefits many people. Having read a lot about him he has really influenced the way I want to live.

Mahatma Gandhi was assassinated in 1948 after a life that led to India's independence from Britain. He has inspired other people to be activists using peaceful resistance. Martin Luther King used the same basic methods.

To me, one of the most important things about him is that he created change in the world from his viewpoint. He was a spiritual man who did political and cultural things to make the changes he wanted. He spent most of his life trying to learn truth. That is basically what we are doing by trying to understand our spiritual side and how that works in the material side.

I try to model my search for truth after him and others I've read about. Gandhi thought it was important to learn from his own mistakes and then apply the lessons to what went on in the future. He said that one of his biggest problems was learning how to defeat his own demons and fears.

I created mine. Because I didn't know how to handle those back then, I kept facing them over and over until I started to learn. I had to push through my fears and remember the lesson that I learned last time I went through the same experience. Then, the next time it would be easier, like every time Gandhi stood up to the British authority.

Some of you may have seen the movie that was made about Gandhi's life by Columbia Pictures in the early 1980s. It is one of my favorite movies. Ben Kingsley won an Academy Award for his role as Mahatma Gandhi.

In one of the scenes, he is in India and is with some workers protesting the conditions they are forced to work in. They are walking down a road toward the place they work, when the British send out soldiers on horseback to run them down and stop the march. None of the workers are armed with anything to protect themselves against the soldiers.

It is horrifying to see the soldiers spur their horses into a gallop and head straight for the workers on foot. Gandhi is in front with others. One of the men with him says to lie down in the road, road the horses won't trample them as they are trained not to do that.

I'm sure they were very scared and thought they would be killed, but they did lie down. The horses couldn't be forced to walk on top of the people in the road. The Indians wouldn't get up, and the soldiers finally had to go back to where they came from. Gandhi knew that the physical part of him might be killed under the horses' hooves, but he lay down anyway with the others. His real power was in his spirit and convictions.

We probably aren't in that kind of life-threatening situation, but the same principles can be applied to our lives. I found that letting go of my attachment to the physical me and relying on the spiritual me is a very powerful way to live.

I learned that others had given him the title of Mahatma, and I looked up what it meant. I found out that it was from Sanskrit words maha, which meant "great," and atma, from the Sanskrit "atman" meaning "soul." According to his biography, he never really thought of himself that way. He just did what he believed in and remembered that we are more than what we see. We are spiritual beings.

His example was to demonstrate integrity between what he believed and how he acted out the thoughts in his mind.

"As soon as we lose the moral basis, we cease to be religious. There is no such thing as religion overriding morality. Man, for instance, cannot be untruthful, cruel, or incontinent and claim to have God on his side."

– Mahatma Gandhi

One of the things I learned from my studies about Gandhi was that our integrity goes as deep as our spirit. If that is the real me, then my thoughts and actions will reflect the beliefs that come from my core—my spiritual part. Since I learned that I am a spiritual being with connections to God and the universe, I realized that what Gandhi said about men and women being children of God is true. We share some of that same spirit since we are created by God with the same energy and from the same material as the universe.

When I first became a Christian, I studied spirituality from Gandhi's viewpoint. One of the things I learned was that according to the Bible, everyone has spiritual gifts. I think those gifts are part of what we tap into and use to make us more successful in creating what we want. In the last chapter about dreams, we looked at finding what your interests are and then figuring out your passions.

For me, I found that I wanted to help people through sharing my mistakes and experiences. I learned from people who walked paths like the one I was on, and I wanted to share with others who were going through the same things as I did. For me, a part of my spiritual being comes out in my work. Your gift may be that you understand people and can empathize with what they are going through. Maybe you want to be a therapist and help people deal with their problems. I chose to be a life coach. It works for me. I hope it helps others find their paths more easily and that their journey can have fewer obstacles. If we share some of the same obstacles, we can encourage each other and use each other's talents to overcome the problems.

According to New Age philosophy, spiritual growth touches every part of your physical life. You can be empowered to be more than you could otherwise. It also teaches that it's not that we have *access* to our spiritual power, but that we *are* spiritual power. From this point of view, there are three basic steps to the success you want. The process of creating your new reality is made up of thought, words, and action.

While I've been developing my abilities to be the "spiritual me" so that I can be creative, I've also had to learn to be comfortable in my skin. Since we are here on this planet as physical beings, we should learn to be at ease with that. It is generally harder to become aware of our spiritual side. All that said, I still have to operate in this body. My actions are physical ones that build or wait for stepping stones that keep me going along my path.

Just as we use our spiritual gifts, we can use our physical gifts. If you are strong and your neighbor needs help moving some furniture, you can do something as simple as help them lift and carry it. Such action manifests your feelings of being helpful to others. While you're doing physical things for them, you can share your experiences with them in casual conversation. I'm not talking about giving them a lesson in what you've learned, like a professor in a lecture. I'm saying that you can share little nuggets with the other person's permission and be supportive of their needs.

Like Gandhi, it is important for you to be true to yourself and your spirit. Don't do things that go against your natural self. Obviously, that doesn't mean giving in to old habits, but keep working on your new, more positive thoughts and actions.

PERSONAL COACHING ACTIVITY

Look how far you have come! You're halfway through the "tools" section of our trip together. We have become more aware of ourselves, looked at our beliefs and their sources, and discovered our dreams, and now we are working toward putting our passions into action. In this chapter, we have briefly explored the real you – the "spiritual" you.

1. Journal about a negative experience. What happened and who was involved when it happened: where were you, how did things turn out, how did you feel about it? Then, write what part of that circumstance you were responsible for and explain how you attracted that situation to you.

2. Journal about a positive experience. Include the same who, what, when, where, how, and what you felt like as in the first exercise. What made this different? Explain your responsibility for the situation and explain how you attracted this different experience. How can you do this again?

Great work! You've built another stepping stone on your path to success.

CHAPTER

CHOICES

"You have many choices. You can choose forgiveness over revenge, joy over despair. You can choose action over apathy. You hold the key."

– Stephanie Marston

One definition of wealth is possessing choices. The more choices we have, the richer we are. We can stumble through life thinking we have no choices and that we are imprisoned by others who control us. "They" make us act a certain way. "They" keep us from becoming all that we can be. Just who are "they?"

Contrary to this way of thinking and reacting, each of us has infinite possibilities at our disposal. Believe it or not, these treasures are just waiting for you to pick them up. Your imprisonment is of your own making. "They" don't keep you there. You do.

With a clear sense of direction and the right help, you can go anywhere you want. The choices we make determine what our destiny will be. Realize that we all need other people to help us – mentors, positive and encouraging friends, and supportive family. Your struggles and frustrations become possibilities, not obstacles.

---

*"There are three constants in life . . .
change, choice, and principles."*

– Stephen Covey

First, we have a choice as to how we react to any situation. A negative situation can rule us, or we can take charge of our own lives. Many of us go through our entire lives doing nothing but reacting to stimuli from our surroundings and other people. We choose to stay in a place of victimization and blame everyone around us for our circumstances. In my case, I allowed feelings of frustration and defeat to keep me from fulfilling my desires. This is purely a reactive stance.

Therefore, make a conscious choice to become proactive. Instead of waiting for something to happen to you, take action. Use the energy that resonates in your spirit and put it to work for you. Keep your dreams in focus. Repeat your positive affirmations from the exercises we have been doing together. Take responsibility for your own thoughts and actions. What you're thinking should be reflected in your actions. It's like the age old saying that actions speak louder than words.

We can all find excuses for not changing or acting. I've lived through nightmare experiences, but they were a reality and required some kind of action from me. Ultimately, I learned different lessons from each experience. The real challenge is to take the lesson with you, but not the baggage. Your choices can be purposeful and intentional. If you are a constant victim, it is because you choose to be one. If you are like I was, you like sympathy, you want others to feel sorry for you. Responsibility is easier to give to others than to assume ourselves. I know. I've done it. Getting sympathy is the greatest payoff for choosing a victim stance, but it is also shallow and short term. Don't you want long-term payoffs? That is what your dreams represent.

Most of my adult life, I existed in a prison that was of my own creation. The interesting thing about my prison is that it was built from my habits. I stood looking through bars of an unlocked cell. I knew they were unlocked, but I was too comfortable in it. It was familiar. The knowledge that I could get out anytime I wanted to should have encouraged me to escape, but I didn't want to open the door. To tell the truth, I didn't know how to act once outside my cell.

Once again, through my own choices, I found myself buried in problems. Through a chain of events, I struggled to keep my head above water. The feeling reminded me of when we tried to save my friend Kevin but nearly drowned in the process. After living in Bend, Oregon, with my wife, Teresa, for five years, we separated and divorced. My finances were in a shambles, reflecting everything else in my life.

It was too easy to slide back into my old habit of running away from my problems. Even after all that inner work, I found myself turning to alcohol and occasionally doing drug. My strong feelings of inadequacy and failure became overwhelming. I thought I had failed my wife and children.

One day, I gave in to my feelings completely. A panic attack drove me into a corner. I drew up my knees and sat in the dark. My chest grew tight. It was so strong I thought I was having a heart attack. Between the alcohol, drugs, and depression, I was so messed up that my body released an imbalance of chemicals, pushing me toward a total mental breakdown. It scared me enough to call my ex-wife and ask her to take me to the hospital. I was convinced I was dying from a heart attack.

It's when we hit our lowest points in life that we can see the need to make a different choice. Forced to choose my future, I could either continue to sink further into that dark, slick hole, or I could find something to pull myself out of it. That decision, in my desperation, was the first step of the journey I continue today.

Strong decisions are driven by intention. If we say one thing and do another, then we never really intended to do it anyway. Not in our heart of hearts. Intention is aim, while objective is a quality of purposefulness. Most people speak their intentions and say their results fell short. I say our results are our intention. If we are in a bad relationship, a bad job, a state of inner or outer conflict, we actually make more progress and assume greater power by taking responsibility rather than insisting these other "bad" things "just happened" to us. Intention starts internally and ends externally. You make all the choices yourself.

You might ask yourself, "What about all the times I fail?" Look at it through different glasses. Take the lesson. We learn more through our mistakes than our achievements. However, this is not to take away from reaching your goal or obtaining your dream. It feels great. Enjoy it.

The great American essayist, Ralph Waldo Emerson, once wrote, "Trust thyself: every heart vibrates to that iron string." I believe these words deserve repeating; we must trust ourselves. We should grow from every experience. Believe that nothing is impossible if you pursue it with unwavering intention. When we don't trust ourselves or stay focused on what we want out of this life that is positive and good, we delay our rewards. When we explain our failure as something we did not intend, we weaken ourselves and speak falsely.

"The supreme value is not the future but the present. The future is a deceitful time that always says to us, 'Not yet,' and thus denies us. The future is not the time of love; what man truly wants he wants now. Whoever builds a house for future happiness builds a prison for the present."

– Octavio Paz

Look at all of your alternatives. Decide which one serves your purpose best. In my case, I wanted to help others so they wouldn't have to suffer through the same traps I fell into. It's not always easy, but it is possible if it's done one step at a time. Sometimes we look at a situation and want to take the easiest way out, but it results in more obstacles in our path than we started with. If "easy" worked, everyone would be a success.

We allow ourselves to be led from one thing to another. All of us have days when we know exactly what we are going to accomplish before dinner. Then, a random thought sends us on a rabbit trail. We see something that needs attention and turn to take care of it. Next, we uncover another minor task while doing the first. It goes on and on. Suddenly, it's five o'clock and we haven't even started on the main project we wanted to finish.

You don't want to become so set in your plan that you can't address emergencies or people who need your help, but you need to use self-control. Don't lose focus.

In the previous chapter, we talked about tapping into the inner power of your spirit. As part of that, we looked at the conscious and subconscious mind. Our conscious mind is the part that thinks things through and then makes a decision based on both the information available to us and on how we feel about it. We use our brain as a filter to allow and accept certain information as part of the decision-making process.

Let's look at opposites for a few minutes. We look at our choices as being either good or bad. We think that someone is ugly or beautiful. If we go all the way back to our senses, we taste things as sweet or sour. These are all opposites. If we concentrate on the negative side of every choice, then that's what we choose. I can make a choice to live in a shack or a mansion, drive a new car or an old one. Train your mind to look for the good things, and then focus on those and attract them to you.

If you are looking for a new job, don't limit yourself to one that will just give you a week-to-week paycheck because you're afraid there isn't another opportunity out there. See yourself in a good-paying job or create the job or business yourself. It's all about limitations or possibilities. Push yourself to make the choices that are positive. Refuse to be negative. I'm not talking about being unrealistic here. I'm just saying that you should choose to have a positive way of looking at life and your circumstances, and choose to make them better.

"It is our choices that show who we truly are,
far more than our abilities."

– Joanne Kathleen Rowling

Joanne Kathleen Rowling is the author of the popular *Harry Potter* books. She wrote them as a single mother living on subsistence wages in Edinburgh, Scotland. Despite her difficult circumstances, she focused on her dream of being a children's author. If she had accepted the limitations of her circumstances, she never would have become the writer that she is. There are many, many other examples of people who have accomplished and attracted great things, and almost all of them will tell you that their success was the result of rejecting limitations.

Part of making positive choices is keeping a positive attitude. When you aren't sure what your choices are, it could be as simple as deciding to keep your good attitude and looking at the world from that viewpoint. From there, you can attract positive thoughts, people, tools, and experiences to help you progress along your path.

Remember to think in possibilities and not limit yourself in the choices you make. I have limited myself at times, but I've learned to look at everything as an option or choice. I've learned to look at what may seem impossible to some people. In 1895, Lord Kelvin, the president of Great Britain's most prestigious scientific organization, The Royal Society, said, "Heavier-than-air flying machines are impossible." Suppose Orville and Wilbur Wright agreed with him? What if no one experimented with building flying machines and we still were stuck on the ground? Imagine

what our world would be like. It doesn't matter if other people tell you
it can't be done or you can't achieve what you choose to do. Don't make
choices based on other people's doubts.

Maybe it can be done. You won't know if you never try. What others
think is unreasonable is not necessarily true. Just because your mother
doesn't think the Law of Attraction is a part of the universe and has no
effect on people doesn't mean she's right. Actually, lots of people reject the
Law of Attraction because to accept it means they would be responsible for
what their lives have become. Many people aren't even aware of what it is or
how it works in their lives. If you let others make your choices for you, it is
like disconnecting from the Internet: You'll never know what it could mean
to you. If you take the easy way out and just give in to what others think, you
won't be able to realize your full potential. Make the choice that is good for
you and the abundance you deserve will come.

Once you make your decision and know your goal, there will be
small course corrections along your path, as we talked about earlier, but your
focus will stay the same. It is with commitment to your choice that you build
your character. It moves you to action and keeps you positive. Most people
go through life being "involved" but not really "committed." The difference
is like the difference between a wool coat and a fur coat. In a wool coat, the
sheep is involved, but in a fur coat, the mink is committed.

The choice of commitment will unlock your imagination and
creativity. Those thoughts build an image and grow into reality that you
created yourself. You didn't have to wait for somebody else to come along
and tell you what to do or how to do it. You don't have to depend on
someone else to make your choices for you any more; you have the power
inside of you. Let that power be your source of confidence so you can make
the choices you need to.

It is fun and freeing to make choices. You are in control of your own life. Things aren't just happening to you anymore. You're making them happen and attracting them into your life.

However, sometimes people fall into the trap of thinking they can achieve everything they want all by themselves. They push away others who want to help. They turn inward instead of outward for all the answers. Some of the answers can be found through meditation, but we forget that part of the reason we are here is to help each other. If we never let anyone do things for us or mentor us, we have denied them an opportunity to be of service. Realization of that fact is a part of the process. Our opportunities to assist others along their paths will come to us, in turn. I want to help you, not so you will help me, but so you will help others.

Over time, reading has become important to me. It gave me access to things I would have never known. For several years I read every self-help or self-devolopment book I could get my hands on. Today, on the bookshelves in my home, you will find my favorites. They include writings by Wayne Dyer, whose father abandoned him as a child. I felt a kinship with him through his words. As the youngest child of four, I grew up thinking my father didn't care about me. Yet, Dyer became successful and gained a spiritual enlightenment that changed his life.

I looked for other heroes or mentors. I focused on attaining them, and one-by-one I attracted books, seminars, and other people to me. John K. Lynch, who died of cancer, was one of my models. His expertise was in network marketing.

I admire Mahatma Gandhi and his philosophies. He was not only a politician, but also a spiritual leader that everyone can learn from. He never lost sight of his goal to help other people, whether he was without shelter, in prison for his convictions, or meeting with the British and Indian leaders of the time. Gandhi once said, "My life is my message." He advocated change through nonviolence. That appealed to me. I'd been in too many fights in my life and wore the physical scars to prove it.

I look up to Oprah Winfrey overcoming many things in her life, she maintains her integrity and always tries to help others. She is considered one of the most influential women in history, as well as a major philanthropist of the 20th and 21st centuries. Her Angel Network encourages people around the world to help each other and is an inspiration to me.

Some of my other favorite authors are Bob Proctor, Steven Covey, Anthony Robbins, and Zig Ziglar. One of the most recent books I've added to my collection is Wayne Dyer's new book, *Being in Balance*.

I started attending seminars led by Bob Proctor and others. I met Paul Martineli at one of them. Learning more and more about my spiritual potential and the Law of Attraction opened new possibilities to me. People of the same philosophy were attracted to me. As my sphere of contacts and friends expanded, so did my efforts to help others.

My relationships with others grew stronger. Reaching and helping other people remained my burning desire. The longer I stayed on this path, the more joyous things came to me. My attitude and focus changed, and I attracted Bob Proctor and Paul Martinelli and their guidance into my life. They helped me find the tools I needed to find complete fulfillment and potential.

I attracted a woman named Janet into my life, and she is now my wife. She is an amazing supporter and has helped me unlock more of my potential than I ever could have alone. Janet has taught me that it isn't about doing everything yourself. It's about building relationships with people who are willing to help you out stand behind you. My well-established habits of doing everything myself took time to break. At first, it was hard to participate in group activities and enjoy the benefit of sharing responsibilities with others. Then, I realized that it is a matter of sharing support and encouragement with each other. Eventually, it occurred to me that this is actually how we are supposed to live.

One last aspect to look at before we go on to the coaching activities is setting your priorities. Decide which steps come first. What are the most important things you want to do?

I heard a story about a college professor who stood in front of his class one day and told the students to watch and observe. He took a large mayonnaise jar, one of the big ones you can get at a discount store. It was washed and empty. First, he put as many two- inch diameter rocks into the jar as it would hold. He asked the students, "Is the jar full?"

They all agreed that it was.

Then the professor took small pebbles and poured them into the jar filling up spaces around the stones. He asked, "Is the jar full now?"

Again, the classmates agreed, "Yes."

"I thought you said it was full before," he said.

The teacher leaned down behind the table and lifted up a small bag of sand. He poured it into the open mouth of the mayonnaise jar, shifted it around, and the sand filled up every, tiny empty space. He looked back at his students. "How about now? Is it full?"

"Yes."

He stood a moment and looked at them all. Then, he took the jar and emptied it out into a box. Next, he took another bag of sand and poured all of it into the jar until the grains of sand touched the lip. A little bit of sand ran over the top and spilled onto the table. For the fourth time, he asked his students, "Is the jar full?"

They all agreed that this time it was truly full.

As the professor nodded and leaned back against the table, he asked, "Do you know what the difference is?"

Everyone sat in their seats silently.

He explained, "If you put the sand in first, there isn't any room for the pebbles or the stones. If you think of the sand grains as the little things that happen everyday and the pebbles as the things you need to do but that aren't that pressing, then the stones are the important things that need attention. If you don't handle the stones first, there is no room for them in the jar."

While I'm making choices and considering the actions to take, I need to prioritize. I handle the stones first, then the pebbles, then the sand. One of the great things about applying the Law of Attraction to my choices is that while I'm paying attention to the stones and keeping focused on filling the jar, the universe has the pebbles and sand waiting in reserve for me. So, when I'm ready for them, they will be there for me to use.

PERSONAL COACHING ACTIVITY

Keep up the good work. I know it's hard to take a look at yourself in the mirror and deal with all those things you've been ignoring or running from, but believe me, it is worth it. If you stumble over something, just pick yourself up and continue down the path you've started.

1. Make a list of positive and supportive people you can spend time with or would like to be with. It's alright if it is a short list to begin with, even one person or a mentor will make a difference. You will attract more to you.

2. Considering the previous chapter's coaching activities, make a list of things you want to change about yourself or your lifestyle.

3. Meet with at least one of the people on your list within the next seven days for coffee, and share with them your list of changes. Ask them to be your accountability partner. You will check on each other to see how you are progressing with your goals. Be a positive force in each others lives. Don't spend time with negative people.

Your stepping stones are growing into a path with direction. Don't give up. Keep on keeping on.

CHAPTER 7

GRATITUDE

"It has been found by experience that a person increases his blessings by being grateful for what he has. Gratitude even on the mental plane is a great magnet. When gratitude is expressed from the spiritual standpoint, it is powerfully augmented."

– Charles Fillmore

We've been discussing positive thinking and attitude. Living with an "attitude of gratitude" can make all the difference in your world. If we lose sight of it, we give up our focus and our purpose. To do the things I love to do and help others unlock their potential is my purpose. Every morning, I sit on the edge of my bed and say out loud, "I am so grateful for this day." Want to know why? Because each day is a gift. It isn't owed to me, and when I go to sleep at night, the next day is never promised to me.

Every day we wake up is another blessing. I am thankful for those things I see and have, but also for things that are coming to me in my life. You will release the poisons in your system with this kind of attitude. If you harbor resentment, it builds up inside of you. You're the one who pays the biggest price, not the person you're upset with. They may not even be aware of your resentment, or they may choose to ignore it. Some people actually take pleasure in your resentments and failures. Avoid them. They are not you, and they are not for you.

Dwelling on circumstances that aren't going your way builds negative energy. It adds poisons to your mind and body. The obstacle that stops you from becoming the person you want to be grows larger from negativity. Learn to be thankful in all things. You don't have to remain stuck in your discomfort or pain. Begin by being grateful for little things.

If you find yourself in a thought pattern that keeps pulling you down into that old black place, think of one small thing you are glad to have. It might start with, "I'm thankful for a cup of coffee this morning," or "I'm glad the sun came up again." Then say out loud to yourself anything that comes to mind or which you are grateful.

You don't like your boss? Be thankful for your job and for the possibilities in your future for the better job you will attract. Talk about your future with your mentor, friends, and family. It's not the *someday* that so many people talk about. You can visualize yourself taking an interview and being hired for the job you truly want, and still be grateful for what your present job is doing for you. At the very least, having a lousy boss is a good lesson in what kind of a boss you aren't going to be.

Gratitude is recognition of your gifts. Again, gratitude is also a verb, not just a noun. It requires action from us. The seed of your actions begins with your thoughts. You can ask for and attract good things into your life.

"First Agreement: Be impeccable with your word. Speak with integrity. Say only what you mean. Avoid using the word to speak against yourself or to gossip with others. Use the power of your word in the direction of truth and love."

– Don Miguel Ruiz

One of the biggest challenges in being thankful is the energy we carry in the old tapes playing in our heads. We forget that all the experiences in our past, positive and negative, make us who we are today. It is how we handle them. Do we choose to continue to poison ourselves, or do we expel the toxins by developing a new attitude of gratitude?

As I read more and raised my level of understanding through newly gained knowledge, my thinking process shifted. I started to comprehend the concept that I had control over my own thoughts. What I put into my brain is what's played back to me. The more tapes and CD's of my favorite inspirational writers and speakers I listened to, the more these new patterns of thinking developed in my physical brain, as well as in my conscious thoughts and speech. I continued to devour books to help me learn and internalize the Law of Attraction, to help me see the possibilities of abundance that surrounded me, and to complete the shift in my new perspective of myself.

I've heard the old saying "garbage in, garbage out." If that is the case, then what I put into my mind did determine what I saw as my results. How I act when faced with an obstacle is up to me, not the obstacle. Even though

I changed my way of thinking, the problem still seemed to loom large over me. The difference was that my perception changed. I changed from inside. I let my spirit out and practiced being grateful for all experiences. Sometimes I needed to remind myself, but it became a new habit.

The process led me to a place of better understanding the role of gratitude in my daily life. My new way of thinking released a power to see things in a brighter light. One of my favorite affirmations is to say, "This is the greatest day ever because my feet are above ground and I am alive and well." Every morning, I begin my day with this saying.

The more I studied about gratitude and how it could affect my future, the more amazed I felt.

I found out that an attitude of gratitude is possible for all of us. It doesn't really depend on genetics. Everyone can develop this attitude. If you've experienced difficult times as a child, you can still become a grateful person. We all seem to have a set of positive characteristics and a set of negative ones, so we can choose to use either one. It all depends on how we look at our past and present experiences. Were they "good" or "bad?" By the way, deciding if something is "good" or "bad" is a "critical judgment" that we are taught to make. (If you really want to liberate yourself, stop labeling everything you see and everyone you meet with "good/bad" labels. I use the terms throughout this book to make the material easier to understand, but in truth, I no longer view events as "good" or "bad." They're just events.)

I had to find a balance between knowing that I could attract good things into my life and being aware that good things can also come my way through other people. If I get out of balance with that, I have a hard time being grateful to others for what they do.

Here's a powerful example of an attitude of gratitude. I once met a woman who had survived an abusive marriage. After almost 10 years, she finally got past her fears and left. She went to a shelter with her children, and then moved to a different town. She told me she had to learn how to put things in perspective. She wasn't thankful for the abusive relationship she had been in, but after counseling and self-help books, she knew that her children were her greatest blessing.

Most of us look at the world in one of two ways. Unfortunately, more of us see failures, trials, and disappointments. We get in the habit of staying in that mindset. This colors our view of the future, so when we think about the future, we see only more of the same. The future is filled with more hassles to endure, more disappointments, and other problems to solve. We hear people say, "Life is a bitch, and then you die," or "Life is a vale of tears." How depressing.

Others look back and see joy, success, and experiences that enriched their lives. It could be twins looking at the same things but from two different viewpoints. There is a story about two men in prison. They spent 23 hours a day in their cells. Each lived in a solitary cell with a solid door. One hour a day, they could walk alone in a small exercise yard. Both cells had a small window on the outside wall overlooking their private exercise space. One man looked out and saw mud; the other looked out and saw stars.

The person who looks back on his life and sees things in a positive way will see his future as one of satisfaction and success. It all starts and ends with the attitude of gratitude. Being grateful is one of the quickest ways I've found to start the Law of Attraction working in my life.

Int he coaching activities at the end of this chapter, you will be given a chance to look at what you are thankful for, but you might want to start keeping a journal to help you notice the blessings in your life. It shouldn't just be a list of things that make you happy, which is okay, because you can learn to be grateful even in tough times. Remember, it is the attitude we're after.

To me, concept of gratitude doesn't mean that I have to be happy in every circumstance. Like the abused woman, it doesn't mean staying in destructive situations, but it does mean finding something to be glad about. Some people might think that this new attitude can make you passive and more willing to be victimized. That isn't what I'm trying to say. If your surroundings and your friends need to be changed for you to have a better life, then by all means do what you need to. I did. You can, too, with the help of others to support you. But everything that comes to us can be used for our own betterment, and we can always be grateful for it if we choose.

In my reading and searching, I also learned that gratitude is tied to our spiritual growth. It is fine to want material things and a good income, but if we get too overwhelmed with those things, it is hard to reflect on ourselves and our actions. It's difficult to keep things in a balance of spiritual and physical harmony. We can easily get sidetracked and think the world revolves around us when, in fact, life is a shared experience with those around us, those that we care about.

A simple way to adopt an attitude of gratitude is to say a short prayer of thankfulness at meals. It can be spoken out loud with your family, or silently to yourself. It acknowledges the fact that you have something to eat. Start with simple things, and your awareness of all the gifts you have in your life will become clearer.

Personally, I admire Mother Teresa. What an example of service to others she was during her life — and still is to many people around the world! She had a great sense of opportunity and thankfulness. Most of us don't see the world the way she did. She went into some of the worst conditions on Earth to help other people. But she was rich in the opportunities that she saw to make a difference in others' lives. From her viewpoint, she was thankful that she could do something for the forgotten and starving people in the streets. It gave her purpose.

As I learn and experience more in being able to help people through the lessons of my own past, I realize that I, too, am given many, many possibilities. I am the one that needs to decide to take the action needed and move forward. I realize that it is a choice to have gratitude as one of the main focuses in my life.

When we go through difficult times, we can learn to be thankful that we have the strength to get through them. It helps us get over things and move on. Hard times are only temporary. It's helpful to remember that little nugget. The good thing about being grateful when things are going well is that it helps us appreciate it all the more when things go wrong. Psychologists have discovered that people share this in common: No matter what we think of our own problems, most of us would rather have ours than someone else's.

Scientific researchers and religious leaders agree that the well-being and health of a person relates to gratitude and the role it plays in their lives. All the major religions agree that it brings reciprocal blessings to you. It is appealing to our emotions and encourages us to be kind to each other.

I recently came across a study by Dr. Michael McCollough of Southern Methodist University in Dallas, Texas, and Dr. Robert Emmons of the University of California, concerning the effect of gratitude on people.

They had three groups of more than one hundred each. The first group kept a diary of things that happened to them during the day. The second group kept a record of negative experiences. The third group wrote down the things that they were grateful for during each day.

At the conclusion of the study, McCollough and Emmons found that the gratitude group felt more loved and were more likely to do kind things for others and receive the same treatment. They felt more alert, enthusiastic, optimistic, and energetic. This group made more progress toward reaching their goals. The other two groups had more people who experienced depression and stress. One other thing they found was that the act and feeling of gratitude was not necessarily connected to any one religious group.

"To educate yourself for the feeling of gratitude means to take nothing for granted, but to always seek out and value the kind that will stand behind the action.
Nothing that is done for you is a matter of course.
Everything originates in a will for the good, which is directed at you. Train yourself never to put off the word or action for the expression of gratitude."

– Albert Schweitzer

When I look back on all the experiences I went through as a child, traveling alone and being on my own as a teenager, I can see that a lot of my problems were because of my attitude. To change your outlook doesn't happen just because your mother or father tells you to get a new one. It took me a long time to develop the "I don't care" and "Don't push me" attitudes I carried around all the time. To make it worse, I blamed everyone else for my bad attitude.

At the time, I had no idea that my lack of gratitude and my defensive attitude caused so many of my problems with people. I got into bad situations that I thought I had to fight my way out of, and then wondered why bad stuff always happened to me. I felt that other people pushed me into behaving badly or made me feel like I needed drugs or alcohol. It took me a long time to learn that what I thought and what kind of attitude I showed to everyone around me made a huge difference in my life. Only a victim says, "You made me mad!" The accountable stance is, "I'm mad about what you did." That way my anger is *MY* behavior, no matter what the other person does. Only then can I learn what I'm really after in getting mad at others.

Since I've been on this path of enlightenment and bringing positive things into my life, I have learned that my attitude has a lot to do with my experiences. It is more important how you respond to something than what happens to you. You get to choose whether you have a bad attitude or one of gratitude.

Indeed, your attitude is more important than your experiences as a child, at school, in sports, or at home. It is more important than what has happened to you in the past, how much money you made from your last job, or how big your house used to be. It's more important than whether you've had failures or successes. It's not just how you dress and what car you drive, or how skilled you might be at something. It centers on your attitude. If it is one of gratitude, you are always thankful for something. That creates positive energy and helps you attract abundance, for now and the future, regardless of your past.

The really good thing about your attitude is that you get to decide what kind you want. You have complete control over how you act and what you learn from it. Every day when I get up, I choose to be grateful for my family and blessings. You can, too.

If we depend on others or blame them for our attitudes or moods, we give up our own power to create things from within our spirit. Other people are going to act how they want to, and we don't have to be controlled by them. We can decide to have a grateful attitude about things, no matter what.

I've learned over the years that life is partly what happens to me. Most of it is how I react to what happens. Instead of making me feel bad or angry, I can react to it how I want to. I can find the thing in the experience that is the lesson or the blessing, and be thankful. Believe me, if I can change my attitude from the dark places I used to spend all my time in, you can, too. You are in charge of what your attitude is every day. It's not anybody else's fault. Don't let other people tell you how to feel or how to act. Develop the attitude of gratitude. It will be a blessing for you, and you will have a more abundant life.

If you have gratitude in your daily life, you will be much happier. You can walk around feeling miserable, or you can be happy and a stronger person. It takes as much effort to be miserable as happy, so why not just choose to be thankful?

You might think it sounds strange to say that the work is the same for both attitudes, but look at it this way: it takes the same amount of energy to say something nice as it does to say something mean. I've found that it usually takes more energy to stay negative when good things are happening than it does to stay positive when bad things are happening.

This change in the way you think is not automatic. It will take some effort on your part, but it is well worth it. Like playing a sport or a musical instrument, the more you practice, the better you become. It will unlock potential inside you that you may not suspect is there.

"There is no scarcity of opportunity to make a living at what you love. There is only a scarcity of resolve to make it happen."

– Wayne Dyer

To move forward in your path, you need to move from thoughts, to words, and on to feelings, and finally actions. When you're moving forward, it is with a positive and thankful attitude that starts in your mind — your spirit. You look for ways to accomplish something you want rather than being stuck on negative thoughts. You choose not to just sit down and say to yourself that what you want can't happen. It can be done. There are steps to get what you want. Gratitude for what you are and have is an important part of that process.

Some people don't understand the idea of being thankful for something you don't even have yet. We've talked about visualizing your dreams. Think about each thing that you will do to accomplish that goal. See yourself reading and listening to self-help books that can help you on your path. Be thankful that these books are available. Don't get caught up in lack. So what if you don't have the books in your house? Go to the library or share with a friend. Go on the Internet. Oh, you just had a negative thought: "I don't have an Internet connection right now," or "I don't have a computer." Go to a friend's house and be thankful you get to use theirs. The library and Internet cafes have computers you can use. Most of all, be grateful for the options.

You live in an abundant world with more things available to you than you can imagine. They are there for you to use and to have.

You may be thinking, "Dean, you don't know what I've been through. You're different. It's easy for you to attract wonderful things into your life and the money for what you want." That, my friend, is a negative way of looking at things. You are coming from a place of lack and hopelessness. Go back to the chapters and the coaching activities. We are building a path together, so that you can get away from those thoughts that pull you back down into dark places. If I can learn and grow past my experiences, you can, too. This book helps you on that path. Stay with me. Don't give up.

I know we can't always control what happens to us. Some experiences are the result of what others around us do; they are just circumstances beyond our control, because we are a part of their circle of life. The big difference I want to share with you is that you have total control of how you react and what kind of attitude you are going to have about it. You get better at it with practice. Soon, you will be in charge of the changes going on in your life, instead of having changes put on you from outside. Scott Hamilton, the Olympic skater, overcame physical problems in his life. He once said, "The only disability in life is a bad attitude."

It is all about deciding to have a positive and grateful attitude. You bring it to your life and share it with others. It's not about negative experiences or things that life brought to you in the past. It is your state of mind. Your mind decides on the attitude you bring to everything.

The more you learn to be thankful, the easier it will be to see things you can be grateful about. Back when I was jobless in Arizona and living in the back of that old pickup with Teresa, I didn't think there was anything to be thankful for. Looking back on that, I can see the things I should have been thankful for. Can you see times like that in your life? It really is your mindset that gives you a different way of looking at things with new eyes and a new perspective. I'm sure you've heard the saying, "Hindsight is always 20/20." It's easier to see things more clearly from the past if we get rid of old, negative energy. Then we can look at it with gratitude. It was an opportunity for us to learn a lesson we need to be able to make our lives better.

Don't concentrate on what you don't want, but on what you do want. Put in writing your own affirmations about what you want. Write them down from the viewpoint of being grateful, as if they are already in your life.

If you're having trouble getting started, let me suggest a dream, and then you can apply it to yours. You see yourself wearing expensive clothes from an exclusive shop, custom-made Italian shoes, driving the newest Lexus model, and staying in a hotel suite for $1,000 a night. Picture yourself doing those things. You pay for the room in cash, in advance, from your new business, which is doing very well. Now, say you are grateful for your new business that allows you to go shopping for the clothes you always wanted but didn't have before. Be grateful for your comfortable, custom-made shoes and for the luxurious leather seats in your new car. The hotel suite and getaway is a gift to yourself for working hard, and you deserve it. Try it.

The attitude of gratitude will make a huge change in how you feel when you get up in the morning and when you go to bed at night. It is in your reach to develop and use gratitude in your everyday life.

PERSONAL COACHING ACTIVITY

For this activity, we are going to look at the present and visualize the future and what you will attract.

> 1. Write a list of all those things, people and experiences for which you are grateful. Look around you and start with the physical things you can see - family, people you know, things in your home - and expand outward from there. Keep this list and add to it throughout the next three days as you think of other things you are thankful for.
>
> 2. Now, this part should be fun. Let your spirit out to play and be creative. Look back at your dreams. You may have other things to add to them. Make a list of those things or people that you will attract over the next six months and express gratitude for each one.
>
> 3. Next, make a list of people, things and experiences you will attract in the coming year. In five years. Keep these and look back on them at least a couple of times a week for a few minutes. Continue to focus and express your gratitude for them. Visualize them in your mind. See yourself doing them.

This is a big one in the process. It may surprise you at first how different your world becomes when you adopt this new attitude of gratitude. Learn to enjoy it.

CHAPTER 8

BELIEVE

"All we have to do is to receive what we are given...
We are given the naturalness to love someone,
to be calm in crisis, to ignore self-defeating
suggestions, to be pleasant, forgiving, tender,
helpful, unworried, brave, energetic."

– Vernon Howard

We hold ourselves back from an abundant life by holding onto the belief system we learned in early childhood. You could be leading a highly successful life and enjoying your journey. Believe in yourself. Easier said than done? That's why we have been building up to this step in the previous seven chapters.

Like faith, belief is confidence that something is true. A deep belief is not necessarily in what you can see and touch, but in what you don't see. At the beginning of our dreams, we don't always see the finished product. In our mind's eye, we may visualize it in great detail, and the more we focus on it, the clearer we make the pictures in our minds. Now, we must believe that it will become real.

The beginning of creating your dreams is the image in your mind. Open the windows of your imagination. Each time a piece of your dream becomes a reality it reinforces your belief in yourself that you can create all of the good things you want in your life. You are attracting them. It's a process of experiencing success at creating the life you want and attracting positive people who will help you realize your dreams. One of the ways we build faith in ourselves is by looking back on our successes. Even the tiny early ones show a track record to refer to when that old obstacle called doubt shows up. Doubt is nothing more than negativity.

Make a conscious effort to maintain positive activities. Your intentional decisions give your actions purpose. Purpose is rooted in your beliefs.

As I made the changes to my outlook and beliefs, I decided I wasn't satisfied with the income I was making. When I first started making six-figures, I thought I had arrived. That thought process only limited me. I had an idea to make a million dollars a year.

At one of the Bob Proctor seminars I attended, he said that if you can hold it in your mind, then you can hold it in your hand. I visualized what I would do if I were making that kind of income. Then I took it from thought, to emotion, to belief in myself and the vision of what could be. I imagined how I would feel. I saw myself doing things as though I already earned a million dollars a year.

About that time in my personal journey, I attended the Science of Getting Rich Seminar and met Paul Martinelli. I thought I was only going to a great seminar to help me along my chosen path. I had been studying the material for four years.

On arrival and check-in, I chose a seat in the back of the room. I'd never met Paul and had no idea who he was. He approached me during the seminar and asked if I had any interest in becoming a consultant with LifeSuccess Productions, the company that Bob and Paul own. The next thing I knew, I was on a plane to Florida for consultant training.

It began with my idea to make a million dollars a year. My visualization, belief, and actions reflecting that idea set up a chain of events, which put me squarely on the path to realize the dream. I would be making a million dollars doing the thing I love most to do: helping others through the pitfalls and obstacles of life to find the true potential within them and making dreams come true.

Staying positive banishes doubt. I learned to develop confidence and belief in my own power to create my dreams. It became a heart issue. As my self-esteem grew stronger, I tapped into my spiritual energy. I learned to love myself and others. The more love you have in your heart, the more it develops the other attributes of faith, hope, desire for a better life, and belief.

In scientific experiments, a belief is used for the basis of an action taken. It works the same way with us. You become more confident in your abilities.

---

*"Belief consists in accepting the affirmations of the soul;
unbelief, in denying them."*

– Ralph Waldo Emerson

One of the ways we can defeat ourselves is to fall into the trap of thinking from the standpoint of what we don't have. I said I believe that I can make a million dollars a year. If I come at that from an awareness that abundance exists for anyone that wants it, then I am much more likely to succeed. If you are someone who made $30,000 last year and you think, "Gee, I wish I could make that kind of money," you are coming from a mindset that emphasizes what you don't have.

The universe is full of possibilities. People have let themselves be trapped in wanting something they believe they will never have. Part of our way of thinking is because of the concepts taught in economics. Even if you never took an economics class in school, you learn the ideas by what you experience. It rests on the principle that something scarce is more valuable than something plentiful, all other things being equal.

In school, we may have learned that if one person does really well on a test, then others won't. Remember when your teachers curved the grades on a test? If one person did really well, that meant that you didn't, unless you were that one child that everyone else was mad at for doing well. If our football team wins in the playoffs, someone else has to lose. We believe that everything is win-lose. It plants in us the belief that everything is scarce. Only a few can do well.

We try to apply that same thought process to everything. We believe that certain jobs, incomes, cars, houses, and boats are available to only the few who can afford them. We get caught in the "paycheck-to-paycheck" mindset. Some of us never have any savings and think we never will. We worry about the future because of all the things we think we don't have today and are sure we won't have tomorrow. I'm sure this is an all-too-familiar thought process.

From what we've been taught in the past, we believe that if someone else succeeds it is somehow at someone else's expense, and maybe our own. Then we take that thought and decide that if we are successful, then others may have suffered for it. This isn't necessarily true; although there are people who amass considerable fortunes that way, but we think that's the only way. Unless you have actually done something to someone else in order to step on them to reach your goal, you have not cost anyone anything. Think of it this way: If you deliver value for the value you receive, you haven't enriched yourself at their expense; you've only worked a fair trade. Now, suppose you are in a position to deliver a lot of value to a lot of people for a lot of value received. You can get rich that way.

Let's look at some things that have changed over the last 10 years or so. Remember when no one thought of buying drinking water? We just went to the faucet in the kitchen or bathroom and got a drink. I remember drinking out of the hose in the backyard as a child. As long as we have rain and snow, don't we have an abundance of water available to us?

Now we buy bottles of water at the grocery store. We wouldn't dream of drinking from a public water fountain or from the bathroom faucet if we had our own bottle of Dasani with us. Okay, I know there are concerns about pollution and chemicals that have comtaminated the drinking water supply, but come on. I suspect that the people who developed water sold them are doing very well. They saw what was coming and used the resource available to everyone, and now they are making money with it.

How many brands of water are there on the shelves of your local market? Five or six? Maybe more? Who would have thought you would go into a store and pay $1.50 for a 12-ounce bottle of water? So, now most of us are paying for something that is actually abundant.

When I took a seminar with Robert Kijosaki, he taught people about making your money work for you. I found I could choose to live from hand to mouth and not have any savings, or I could learn the skills that would show me how to tap into abundance that I hadn't thought available to me 15 years ago. I've moved from a viewpoint of believing that I would always be broke or working for someone else, to working for myself doing what I love and making a good living at it.

The money I put into savings I can invest to get a higher rate of interest or even compound interest. I'm not going to go into money management and interest here, but those are skills that I found available to me. I can choose to invite abundance into every aspect of my life.

The way you consider the possibilities open to you for a million-dollar income is ruled by what you believe about yourself. If you're still thinking that you don't deserve it or can't really achieve it, you have limited yourself with your same old negative beliefs. That's one of the things we're trying to change.

"I bargained with life for a penny,

And life would pay no more,

However I begged at evening

When I counted my scanty store.

For life is a just employer

He gives you what you ask

But once you have set the wages

Why, you must bear the task

I worked for a menial's hire

Only to learn dismayed

That any wage I had asked of life

Life would have willingly paid."

– Jessie B. Rittenhouse

This poem is a good example of how most of us approach our world. It is always from a position of what we don't have. If you look around you, there is abundance everywhere. In the sky, there are more stars and galaxies than you can count. The universe is always expanding, according to scientists. How can that represent anything but abundance to us?

There are more books in the library than you can read in a lifetime. If you love to go out and eat, you will never run out of places to go. You may say there are only 50 restaurants in your town, but what about the towns around you?

Think about a more "down to earth" example. A friend of mine is a gardener. Several years ago when she started some new flowerbeds in her yard, she went to the store and bought packages of seeds and some small plants to get her started. At the end of the growing season, she collected seeds from the dried blooms and had several Zip-lock bags full of seeds to plant the next year. That's abundance. One year, she planted tomato plants, and some of the tomatoes fell on the ground and the birds ate them. They left behind some seeds, and those seeds came up as volunteer plants the next year. She ate tomatoes from those bushes. Pecan trees dropped nuts that the squirrels buried, and then sprouted to grow another tree. Trees, bushes, flowers, and food are abundant on our planet.

You can have any part of this that you want. If you have a skill to share with others or lessons you think are valuable to others, I promise there are people who want to learn from you. You will never run out of people to share with. You are only limited by your belief that you don't know anyone or that you don't believe you have anything to say. Forget those negative feelings and thoughts; they aren't true.

When I started to realize my dream of helping others, it began small; the more I focused on it and the more I believed in myself, the more people I reached. After awhile, I not only spoke to my own congregation on Sundays, but also to other churches who asked me to come and be a guest speaker. Then, groups that were not churches wanted to hear my story and wanted me to speak to them. Each time I did, I felt that much better about myself and believed I was capable of helping others. I didn't get stuck in those old tapes from my middle school speech class. That was in the past, and I am a totally different person than the boy who couldn't do it. Now I speak in public all the time and enjoy it. I enjoy the contact with other people who are looking for the same things I am.

I know that everyone has heard about meeting someone who you feel is a kindred spirit and shares your beliefs. Well, since I've been on this path, I've met more and more. Talk about abundance— that's part of it, too.

I told you about my family and my wife, Janet. We believe in each other and in the path that we are traveling together. My family's support for me to realize my dreams has grown continuously over the past several years.

A woman I talked to not long ago told me that she had always wanted a big family. That was her dream. She came from a family with only two children. She had only a few cousins scattered around the country, and they didn't see each other very often. She wanted a family that would be close. That was her dream.

After a disastrous first marriage, she was a single mother of three children for 10 years. She knew what she wanted but had her doubts about ever finding it. In her mind, she had always seen herself with six children, a loving husband, good friends coming to visit, grandchildren playing in the yard, dogs romping with the children, and big holiday dinners where everyone enjoyed each other's company.

In her mid-40s, she met a man who was divorced. He had three grown children and the same dream. After a couple of years of dating, they got married, and she had what she envisioned. They realized that dream together because they believed it could happen. No, it was not that everything in their lives was always perfect. They faced the challenges of life all of us encounter, but they found a contentment that started with her belief of what she wanted her family to be.

I was thinking about my talk with this woman and others I've talked to, and I realized that most of us only share our thoughts and beliefs about the external things in our lives. We share things like the fact that the world is round, the universe is still growing, the sun rises in the east, and we believe in God. We stay with safe subjects so that we don't expose ourselves and our deepest beliefs. We think if we're lucky we might have a friend or family member we could share our deepest feelings with.

I've found that it's not luck. I have had a part in creating every personal relationship I've ever been a part of. The deep down stuff that we carry around with is difficult to share with others, but it makes a relationship strong when shared with the right person. Looking back at my parents, I'm sure there were times they wondered what it was that made me act like I did. I've learned what part of that I'm responsible for and have been able to put into perspective what part they had in it. The bottom line is that I chose to believe negative things about myself when I was young.

Later in life, I was able to start on this path I'm on, and now I live the future that I created back then. I just keep on looking forward and believing in myself to be the person I want to be. I never let go of my belief that I'm here to help other people like myself. We learn from each other and help each other.

Wayne Dyer says that abundance is always there for us and that we just need to tap into it. One thing about the Law of Abundance that we haven't talked about yet is the aspect that is not monetary or material. These things you can have in addition to creating material dreams.

When we believe we can be successful and are aware of the abundance available to us, we can enjoy that part of the journey. The more you have, the more you share with others, and then the more you have. It is a complete circle. Have you ever noticed that the people who always want something for free are living in a world focused on lack?

If you have a certain talent, you can share that with others. If you're in business, time is literally money for you. You can share your time with others who need to be encouraged and supported in their dreams. In a relationship, when you invest yourself in it, you will enjoy the benefits of having someone to be your friend, your confidant, and soul-mate.

Other factors that are an important part of your belief system and realizing abundance include having a sound mind, being able to think and reason or being able to dream. You may not think of it this way, but good health is part of living an abundant life. If you have been through times of sickness or injury, then you know the value of good health.

I heard about a young man who had a bike accident when he was in his early 20s. He had always been strong and athletic, but it took him about three years to fully recover from catastrophic head and neck injuries. He had a severe concussion with swelling of his brain, a broken neck and back, and he developed bad headaches. He was used to being outside riding his mountain bike, climbing, hiking, skiing, and snowboarding, but literally overnight he was in a coma in an ICU.

During the healing process, the doctors told him he couldn't do those physical things that he loved so much for at least a few months. At first, he was depressed and disappointed. Later, when he went back to his basic belief system and looked at the opportunities that were available to him while he recovered, he turned to reading and learning new things. He used his natural talents to learn to play a guitar and to start painting. He believed he could still be a valuable person and create the life he wanted, even though he could no longer live that life with the same carefree disregard for danger that he had before.

Since then, he has had a few setbacks, but he is doing some climbing again and often rides his bike. He is healing more every day. He has had a good support system with his wife, friends, and family, but it goes back to his own beliefs. He believes in himself and his ability to heal and have an abundant life ahead of him.

PERSONAL COACHING ACTIVITY

Once again, we are going to look back at your dream list.

> 1. Journal what you look like living out your dreams. Describe how it will feel when you do. Look back on the accomplishments you've made so far. You're building continually through these activities. Congratulate yourself and use this to begin building that belief in yourself and the abilities to accomplish all you want.
>
> 2. Next, look back at your list of attributes. Add to it those things you want to be. Treat them as if they are a reality right now. See yourself behaving that way, gaining confidence. Start acting as if you have already made the change. Keep practicing the ones you already possess. Write in your journal how this makes you feel. Share it with your accountability partner or mentor.
>
> 3. If you don't meet regularly with your partner or mentor, begin keeping a schedule that fits you both. Have coffee together once a week.

Remember, these are all steps in a process. Enjoy the journey. Life is not a destination, it is what happens along your path.

CHAPTER

PERSISTENCE

---

*"Always bear in mind that your own resolution to succeed
is more important than any other one thing."*

– Abraham Lincoln

In your collection of keys to open up your life's potential, one of the most important is persistence. Think of a little child who wants a toy. Children are relentless. Saying "no" to them doesn't even dent their resolve. They are innocent and focused. That toy is the object of their all consuming passion, and they will never give up asking for it until they get their way. We are all born with that quality and use it regularly as children. Somewhere in our process of growing up, we left that behind with our dreams. Go back and pick your dreams up. Hang on to them with everything you have inside you. And while you're at it, pick up that persistence, too.

There will always be people who will tell you it can't be done or that you'll never reach your goals to realize that dream. *Do not listen to them!* Use the tenacity of a child. "No" is only a word. It is not a roadblock.

Nothing in the world can take the place of persistence. Talent will not; nothing is more common than unsuccessful people with talent.

---

*"Genius will not; unrewarded genius is almost a proverb.
Education will not; the world is full of educated derelicts.
Persistence and Determination alone are omnipotent.
The slogan 'Press On' has solved and will always solve the
problems of the human race."*

– Calvin Coolidge

We are born to persist in those things that we want to do. We make time for them, no matter how busy we become in the daily stuff. Look at Lance Armstrong as an example of endurance. In the mid-1990's, he won the Tour de Pont twice and was considered the finest cyclist in the United States. But in 1996, he was diagnosed with extensive testicular cancer, and the medical community gave him less than a 50% chance of surviving treatment.

Cancer stopped him for awhile, but he refused to give in to it. Doctors will tell you that the outlook of the patient can make all the difference in the final results. Armstrong went on to win the Tour de France six times in a row. In his fight with cancer, he experienced setbacks. He felt defeated and depressed at times, but never stayed in those feelings for too long. He kept his focus on doing the things he loved most.

After the debilitating effects of chemotherapy, Lance Armstrong had to start at the beginning to train for racing again. He invested his actions and his emotions in obtaining what he wanted. He never gave up.

You can apply that same tenacity to your life. Lock your focus on what you want and be willing to do what it takes to obtain it. Trip, fall, skin your knee, suffer setbacks, fall flat on your face, but get back up and keep going. You haven't failed unless you give up. If you find yourself going back to old habits that have failed in the past, stop. Refocus and begin again. No matter what happens along the road, visualize yourself at the finish line. This will keep you going in the direction you need to continue.

For the past 26 years, I've pushed through every obstacle in my way. Sometimes that meant struggling with one step forward and two steps back, but ultimately I took more steps in the right direction than I took in retreat. I met people with changed lives and positive attitudes. When I was working at the lumberyard in Arizona, the guys told me their stories. I thought I was somehow unique in my experiences, but found that I was one among many. At first, when they shared their experiences with me, my old habits, defensiveness and rationalizing came out in my conversation, as though I had to apologize for not being more successful.

The other guys were patient with me. At first, I thought they just wanted to convert the long-haired freak that Kim hired. But over time, my defenses lowered, and I related to their experiences. They were like me in many ways. Some of them had been thieves; others had spent time in jail or prison. Others were former drunks and druggies. They built a relationship with me first, and then they invited me to go to church with them. It marked one of the biggest turning points in my young life.

I wanted to help other people like these five guys had helped me. It was a bumpy road in many cases. Sometimes, just when I thought I had what I wanted in my grasp, my dreams would elude me. I kept repeating the same mistakes, but I wanted different results. Finally I learned what I was supposed to be learning from the experiences. Once I got the lesson, I could move on to something else.

Progress toward what I wanted became less elusive. People pointed me in the right direction to get there. Others walked with me and showed me the tools. Now, I am at the place in my life where things are happening so fast that I have to run to keep up, and I feel blessed every step of the way. I'm growing into the person I want to be and getting stronger every day.

"You become what you think about."

– James Allen

I cannot give you persistence, but if you will follow the steps discussed in these chapters, then you can realize that you are a spiritual being with a gift for creating a better life for yourself. After years of struggle, I finally came to know myself. Along the way, I learned that we can choose to live inside our limitations and be trapped by our history, or we can move forward in faith.

Everyone that picks up this book has practiced persistence at one time or another. Think about learning to read. Like me, you kept working at it until you achieved competency. It didn't happen immediately or magically just because you said you wanted it. It was a process. We repeat that pattern over and over with each task we learn to perform.

The first time you tried to cook dinner it probably turned out a total disaster, followed by a trip to the McDonald's. But you tried again and took what you learned the last time in the kitchen, and applied it to the task. Each cooking experience taught you something until you reached the point that you could at least feed yourself and maybe even impress a guest.

Take that same feeling and apply it to your goals and dreams. Make the commitment to yourself and your accountability partner to stay with it. When you think you can't go another step forward, call a friend to help you out and encourage you. In turn, encourage others. As we have said before, you can't do it all by yourself.

Successful athletes and business people have a "never say die" attitude that their competitors can't destroy. They know what they want to accomplish and will do what it takes to get it. As I mentioned earlier in this chapter, as children we know how to hang on to the image of what we want. Then life happens and we let others take that away from us. We learn to think that we are unable to obtain our dreams, even as we noticed there were many other people who did! We give up on the dream of who we want to be. Each story is different, but we all share the same feeling of defeat. We need to get away from that feeling because it defeats us before we even get started.

Here's another example for you to think about. Watching television recently, I saw a show that talked about the Roman Empire and how they built roads everywhere they went. I found out that when the soldiers weren't fighting they were building roads and forts to live in. First they had to dig out the dirt and rocks, clear trees, and survey the land. Archeologists have found that the Roman roads had long stretches that were absolutely straight. They didn't concentrate on making pretty bends around the landscape unless they were forced to go around something that couldn't be dug through. They built bridges over rivers and other obstacles. It is amazing how many parts of those roads still exist after 2,000 years.

The "digging out the base" is like the work we've done to clear away the old tapes and beliefs we had before. It gives us a place to put newer and stronger information that we are learning. The soldiers put a hard packed foundation of gravel and dirt down for the base of the road in order to make the roadbed easier to build on. What they used depended on the materials available around them. When we do the work required to be what we can be, we use the materials available and then go from there. We take the basic concepts of the Law of Attraction, Law of Vibration, and Law of Abundance and pack those in solid. We keep learning until we have what we need to move on to the next level.

Roman roads had a second layer of larger stones and clay or cement. This layer was up to two- feet thick. To me, this is like the learning stage when I was reading everything I could get my hands on and listening to other people to guide me on how to get past any obstacles. However, after I became more aware of myself and my spirit, I learned how to handle my fears and doubts. Then I got my dream cemented in place and began tapping into my spirit to use the power I had in me.

I thought it was interesting that the top layer of the Roman roads was like stepping stones. Each stone was shaped so that it fit with the others, and made a much smoother surface for the legions to travel on. The road was literally a ribbon of stepping stones. That's what we are doing now: building our own steps for the path we want to take.

Roman roads were built higher in the center so that water and other things would run off to the side. That's how we need to be. We need to let the thoughts we don't need just go off to the side and leave them behind.

The other thing the roads had was a curb. It kept the edges of the road from crumbling. That is what happens for us when we focus on the path. It's like the blinders on a horse, in a way.

The Roman Empire built roads all over the known world. They never stopped building. They never lost their focus on the need for clear roads to get where they wanted to go. There is an old saying that "All roads lead to Rome." At that time, the main roads that the soldiers built *did* all lead to Rome. That's how we need to be in our focus and our determination. Through our choices, all of our roads should be leading us to the dream we are trying to make into our reality.

The Roman Empire lasted for a thousand years. If the legend is true, Rome started with two brothers, Romulus and Remus. Their grandfather had been a powerful king whose kingdom was overthrown, so when Romulus and Remus grew up, they built a city that would be one of the most powerful in all of history! Think of it: The Roman Empire began with a thought. There are lots of examples of persistence in history, stories of people who never gave up in spite of the obstacles in their way! Even though Rome is no longer the empire it once was, it is still a powerful, colorful city, and home to one of the most powerful organizations in the world, the Roman Catholic Church.

We succeed or fail by what goes on inside of us. If we've made choices that didn't work out, then we have to learn from them and make the next part of the path stronger.

"My will shall shape the future. Whether I fail or succeed shall be no man's doing but my own. I am the force; I can clear any obstacle before me or I can be lost in the maze. My choice; my responsibility; win or lose, only I hold the key to my destiny."

– Elaine Maxwell

For people who are successful in making their dreams come true, the words "impossible" and "can't" don't play a part in their thinking. They are always looking for solutions to problems and working with like-minded people. They support each other and help each other up when they fall.

Giving up is not an option. Winners are just people like us who may get beaten but never give up. In fact, to the successful people in the world, the only defeat that feels like failure *is* giving up. I don't like feeling that way, and I'm sure you don't either. Persistence is tied to my feelings and acts as an inner motivator to me. I don't see myself as a loser; I do the things that winners do. And I don't stop.

Not every experience on your path will be easy. Depending on what your dream is, there may be outside factors that have a bearing on what your short-term results are. If you want to run a retail store, you know that markets change and seasons change. The months that people are gone on vacation may be slower than the months just before Christmas. You know that is part of being in retail. You plan for the things that may happen, but you visualize what you want and work toward your success.

If you don't think there are ups and downs on every path, then you are being unrealistic. I have gotten caught by that myself when I had my own business in landscaping. I had to work around the seasons. It was just part of the whole picture. If I didn't want to handle that, I needed to choose something else to do. That is what I did. I decided to do something else. I wanted to be a life coach and help others. So that is the road that I am now building.

"Never give in, never give in, never, never, never, never – in nothing, great or small, large or petty – never give in except to convictions of honor and good sense."

– Winston Churchill

Every step may not be easy, but it is worth the effort and determination. Persistence pays off in your success in making your dreams a reality, but sometimes the lesson you learned with the experience is the payoff, a win-win situation. But you have the choice of seeing it as a win and not a failure. You apply what you learned and move on through that obstacle to tackle the next.

No football player has ever made it to the end zone without pushing through the blocks and focusing on the uprights. He is always focused on the points his team will score when he crosses the goal line. The quarterback works his team down the field. The linemen block the "problems" so that the ball carrier can get past them. That's what your supportive friends and mentor are doing with you.

I'm sure everyone has heard their grandparents say, "The early bird catches the worm." This idea comes from when most people lived on farms and had to get up early and start their work. Since they didn't have electricity, that was the only way they could get everything done. If you would rather sleep until noon and then party all night, you may want to look at your goals again. You may need to change your schedule and learn to use business hours to make the contacts you need to be successful. Most of the world doesn't work from one o'clock in the afternoon until five and then party.

If you want to keep doing that, then you need to have a different dream. Maybe the kind of business you need to be involved in is one that can use those hours. There are many possibilities. Just be sure your dream fits your physical rhythm, and if it doesn't, then you'll have to make adjustments in your own schedule to make room for your success.

Remember that using your natural talents will give you the best results. Then you learn what else you need to know in order to change your reality to what you want. I had to change my daily life when I started working in Arizona. I worked certain hours as a minister. Now, I have a totally different schedule as a life coach and speaker. I had to learn the skills I needed and expand my way of thinking.

You need to be willing to invest yourself and your time into having the things that you want. I don't want to overemphasize the work it takes to succeed, but I don't want you to think that sitting around being positive is the only thing you need to do to attract things into your life. It's a combination of thoughts, attitudes, and actions.

If you just stay in one place, you're like the Dead Sea. I called the Dead Sea because nothing lives there. The water is too salty and there is no outlet. The water doesn't go anywhere and it provides little nourishment for the people and wildlife surrounding it. You have to feed your spirit and your mind with the positive information and energy that will keep you going, and you must do something.

In contrast, the Jordan River runs from the north, into the Sea of Galilee. That sea is actually a very large lake and has been used for fishing for centuries. People still fish on it. The fresh water, which includes spring runoff from the mountains, comes into the lake from the river. At the other end of the lake, the river continues south through Israel and finally ends in the Red Sea. Because the Sea of Galilee is always being fed with fresh water, it is abundant with resources. The Dead Sea only receives and doesn't give anything, so it is evaporating and dying. The only real value it has is its salt factories and mineral value. Tourists only visit because of its Biblical significance, not because of its usefulness.

We, too, can be like one of these seas. We keep feeding ourselves with positive information and thoughts that help us, and in turn help other people, too. We can create an abundant world for ourselves and help others realize they can have it, too, if they choose. Or we can do nothing and die, empty and unfulfilled.

I have found that I have to stay committed and continue to push on toward the million-dollar income that I see myself earning. Most people who are able to create their dreams never stop doing the things that it takes. They do the things that successful people do and experience the feelings that go along with that. Sometimes that means being the early bird, and sometimes that means adapting your dream to what you are willing to do. In either case, be willing to do what it takes and to keep going until you've reached the end of the race. If a runner at a track meet only goes 90 meters in a 100-meter dash, it doesn't matter whether he got there first. If he doesn't go the full100 meters he can't earn the prize. Don't be the world's best 90 meter sprinter.

You can create a satisfying and abundant life. However, if you beat yourself up over mistakes, you are making more obstacles for yourself. Be accepting of yourself and realize that you are not always going to do the right thing. What matters is that you keep going and breaking your old habits of thought and action. People who are champions don't keep thinking about the mistake they just made. They never lose sight of the goal.

If a quarterback throws to a receiver in the end zone and the ball is knocked out of bounds by the other team, he can't afford to keep thinking about how he messed up the last play. He has to go into the huddle and forget the mistake. He has to focus and get the other players to concentrate on the upcoming play. If he spends the next 10 minutes beating himself up because he didn't get the ball to the receiver, the game is over and his team will probably lose. With focus, he can throw a touchdown pass the very next play.

Practicing perseverance doesn't mean that you will never have doubts or be afraid along the way, but it does mean that you won't waste time dwelling on them. If you made a mistake the last time you got to this point, be like the quarterback and shake it off. If you keep thinking about it, you recreate what you don't want. If you allow yourself to keep thinking how scared you are, you can't move past it and do what needs to be done. Go ahead and feel afraid, but do it anyway.

Another thing I realized is that at times you need to relax and take a break from your efforts. You need to feed your body, your spirit, and your mind. Like a car has to fill up its tank with gas to run, you have to fill yourself up with more energy. In another chapter, we discussed meditation. Meditation is an excellent way to take a break and get energized. Everybody needs to take a day off and recharge. It makes you that much more prepared to push through the obstacles you meet.

Have you ever noticed that sometimes people are not as satisfied when they get to the end of a journey as they thought they would be? One of the things I have forgotten to do over the years is to enjoy the trip itself. I get so focused on the end result that I forget that part of the happiness available to us is from the journey. I know that every detail may not be fun, but the trip is a great teacher and we can meet supportive and positive people along the way, people who are fun to be with and who want to share their journeys with us.

Think about flying during the holidays. Sometimes you get snowed in at an airport. Instead of yelling at the airline personnel behind the counter because you're mad about the interruption of your plans, think about some positive things that you can do while you're stranded. If you're there with your family it can be a kind of "time out." You could just spend that time talking to each other and catching up on things. If you are by yourself, you can read the self-help book in your carry-on bag that you haven't had time to get to. Meet people around you. Connect with others who are stuck in the same situation. You may attract someone that will change your life, someone you would have never met otherwise.

You don't have to just put on a happy face, but you can take advantage of the time available to you that you didn't know you would have. Look at it as a blessing and enjoy yourself along the road. I found that my life is made up of many experiences, not just steps on a blank road. I can have a good time and like what I see, or I can decide to make myself and everybody around me miserable. As the late John Lennon put it so well, "Life is what happens to us while we're busy making other plans." Life isn't just what we planned to do, life is also the changes in plans that we never foresaw. We have choice about how we live those moments, too.

I know that everyone's path is their own and different from mine, but we do have some things in common. Even if we don't share the same experiences, we at least share common feelings. We can share our hurts and help each other heal. These things make the path better than it could have been. They help us keep going when we're tired and feeling disappointed. This sharing process is exercise for the soul. We are stronger for it.

I can't tell anybody what their path should be, but I want to share what mine has been like and let others know that they aren't alone. You have lots of company. Others feel the same way you do. We can help each other learn how to react better and encourage each other to keep going toward the goal that grew out of our dreams. It isn't impossible, but it takes commitment and persistence. Keep going — I will, too.

One more thing to look at before we go on to the coaching activities is how we know what to do next. In other chapters, I've mentioned that the powers in the universe will work out the picky details, but you also have to be active in the process of choosing the steps you are willing to take. Sometimes people give up before they even get started, because they don't know what to do to take the first step. Sometimes you're halfway there and you get lost because you're not sure what comes next.

Try to keep your overall focus on the long- term goal and dream. If you're stuck where you are, but there are constructive things to accomplish that will bring you farther down the path, then do those. They may be little things like staying organized. Maybe you haven't filed any of the articles you are collecting as learning resources for your project. Spend some time doing that. It is a part of the process of realizing your dream. Go online to look for new books by your favorite authors. You will be learning more that will help you. It may supply your next step, or you may meet someone at the bookstore looking for the same subject. You've attracted those things step in your plan.and people into your life, and you can help one another. It may only be a brief conversation while you stand in the book aisle at Barnes & Noble or your favorite store, but it may be the puzzle piece you need to figure out the next step in your plan.

What do you think the athletes in the Olympics go through to win a gold medal? Most of them started in their sports as young children. Some ice skaters start at 5 years old. Hockey players on the next Olympic team could have started with roller hockey at age six in their hometowns. They watch the pros on television and want to be like them. They practice after school in the driveway with friends. They play pick-up games as they get older with other children in their neighborhoods.

If a boy lives in the same town where there is a hockey team, he may be able to get a job helping around the locker room. He learns from the players. He learns from the coaches of his own team. They have practice a couple of times a week and games on weekends to teach and reinforce both the fundamentals of the sport and the work ethic needed to win.

During the off-season, the boy goes back to playing in the driveway. He doesn't stop working on his game because the season is over. He reads every magazine there is about his sport. He loves it and sees himself getting a scholarship to college to play hockey and then being drafted into a semi-pro team and working his way up. He wants to be just like Wayne Gretzky. At night, he dreams about playing hockey. He hears and feels the crowd going wild when he puts his helmet on and heads out on the ice.

In 1980, the United States put an Olympic hockey team on the ice that no one expected to win. Bill Clement, a Canadian ESPN analyst who played hockey during the 80's, said, "Before then, the criticism of American players was that they weren't tough enough, couldn't score when they had to, and couldn't win big games for you or with you. That mentality changed after 1980."

How's that for an expectation to live down to?

Herb Brooks, an NCAA coach who had played on two Olympic hockey teams, traveled the country holding tryouts and put together Team USA. He worked with the them for a year and a half, and during that time just about every other team in the world beat them badly. Not long before the Olympics in Lake Placid, New York, Team USA played an exhibition game against the Soviet national team and were beaten 10-3.

When the Olympic Games started, the players of Team USA felt confident, but they weren't sure they could get anything above a bronze medal. They tied with Sweden and then beat Czechoslovakia. That started to build up their confidence, but they knew they would have to face the Soviet team again. They still remembered the sound beating they received in the exhibition game.

In their next games, they defeated Norway, Romania, and then Germany in a comeback game with a score of 4-2. The Soviet Union's team was undefeated. That meant that when they got to the medal rounds, Team USA had to play the Russians in the first game. Of course, the Russians came out on the ice and played hard and fast. They were in the lead, 2-1 close to the end of the first period. The Americans fought their way to a 3-2 lead in the last 20 minutes of the game. Then, with only 10 minutes to go, they picked off a Soviet pass and scored on a 25 foot shot. The game ended with a score of USA 4, USSR 3. It was grueling and it was unprecedented, and had the Olympics ended right there, they would have been heroes to America. But they still had to play Sweden, and the winner would get the gold. Team USA won.

What had seemed impossible to most people, the team and their coach had made real. They hung onto their dream through all the months of practice and exhibition games. They kept going even when they were tired and faced the team they most feared. They pushed past their obstacles and did what no other hockey team in America's history had done. They won a gold medal. The whole world considered Team USA an underdog, except the members of the team. Their persistence and teamwork won out. Some of the players, including Neal Broten, Dave Christian, Mark Johnson, Ken Morrow, and Mike Ramsey, went on to become hockey stars in the NHL.

When you move forward, hold a strong belief in yourself and your ability to accomplish great things, and engage the spiritual part of you; a flame of persistence is lit that cannot be extinguished by anyone but yourself.

PERSONAL COACHING ACTIVITY

These activities are meant to take the theories we've discussed and forge them into real stepping stones. Maintain your positive attitude and you will attract others of a like mind.

1. Journal how you see yourself as a success. Include your feelings, the six senses, and what the complete experience looks like as far as you can visualize it. Remember, don't limit yourself. Push your limits. These are meant to be growing exercises, not something to file away on your shelf with your other books.

2. Begin writing a plan for how to accomplish your dream. Write out steps that need to be taken. Discuss and get input from your mentor. Take your time. These exercises don't need to be done in an afternoon. Remember, this is the thing you want most. This will become your reality.

Your plan is just like a road map that you follow to get to your favorite vacation place. Stick with the road, and you will arrive where you wanted to.

CHAPTER

LOVE

*"Love is an attempt to change a piece of a
dream world into reality."*

– Theodor Reik

There have been songs and poems, fiction and fantasy written about love for centuries, much of it written about love lost or never found. It seems the more common human experience is to feel alone, separated from others, and unhappy with our lives. How can something so talked about be so elusive to us? It may be because we forget that we need to love ourselves before we can seek love from others. Wayne Dyer said it this way, "You cannot be lonely if you like the person you are alone with."

Once again, we begin with the person you see in the bathroom mirror. You cannot escape yourself.

After devouring many books about changing my life for the better, I felt like I was gaining more strength as a person. As always, I wanted to help others. Through my own humbling experiences, I knew I could empathize with other people and understand what they were going through.

I did as much on my own as I could but finally went to a therapist. She helped me to put things into perspective and to heal myself. Early in our sessions, she told me that she wanted me to look myself in the mirror every morning and every night. While looking myself in the eye, I was to tell myself, "I love you."

My first reaction was to laugh in her face. Was she kidding? However, she persisted in telling me I needed to do this as a step in the healing process. I needed to learn to love myself. I begrudgingly started the process.

I remember the first morning looking in the mirror feeling stupid and hoping no one could hear me on the other side of the bathroom door. I said, "I love you." I felt like a liar and an imposter. It was a completely alien thing for me to think, much less say. I did stick with it, regardless of my initial reaction. In time I started to change my feelings. I actually fell in love with myself, not narcissistically, throwing kisses to any reflection of myself, but a healthy, normal self-love. Love of self, I learned, is the foundation for loving others in our circle of family and friends as well as others we share this planet with.

It wasn't an easy process. I hit many roadblocks from the years of believing that I was stupid and useless. With the small victories throughout the process, however, I knew I had to stick with it. I didn't want to give up. I felt much better about myself than I ever had before. Healthy self-love became my foundation.

When I was studying the Bible and writing sermons on a weekly basis, one of my favorite books was 1st Corinthians. It gives a great definition of love.

"Love is patient, love is kind. It does not envy, it does not boast, it is not proud. It is not rude, it is not self-seeking, it is not easily angered, it keeps no record of wrongs. Love does not delight in evil but rejoices with the truth. It always protects, always trusts, always hopes, always perseveres ... And now these three remain: faith, hope, and love. But the greatest of these is love."

– The Apostle Paul, 1 Corinthians 13:4-7, 14

Loving others was the next step of my healing. As the years passed, I grew stronger in my relationship with myself, but I also built better relationships with my friends, family, and children. It seemed the more I learned about the spiritual side of my personality, the more I wanted to know. Each day, I found new books to read and tapes of speakers to listen to. I drew strength from them and grew stronger in my resolve to become a better person and help others. I found new hope for my future. I believed in my heart that I could accomplish my goals and attain my dreams. I had learned to love and respect myself and others.

One tough lesson was to let go of old resentments I harbored for my parents, family members, teachers, classmates from childhood, old girlfriends, my ex-wife, and the list went on. When I learned that rolling these negative feelings and tapes over and over in my mind only served to poison me, I started working through it. Counseling helped tremendously, as did the books I read.

Self-love is okay. It is a building block. Your self-esteem grows over time. You are more positive. You attract more positive and loving people to you. Love is not *ego*-driven, it is *other*-driven. When you keep agreements with yourself and others, your self-esteem is fed. Breaking agreements with yourself decreases the positive feelings. Changing your behavior and feelings is a renegotiation with yourself for a better way of living. Loving others is healing for them and for yourself.

Let's look at self-love and try to understand it. Since you need to love and respect yourself first, it's important to know how that works. After all, you can't give away what you don't have. Self-love is essential in learning what love really is and how it can affect your life. Even though it is a key first step on your path, I saved it for last because it is the best. I didn't want the topic to get lost. Learning about self-love can help you make lasting changes in your future.

Your deep feelings about yourself create your self-image and your basic beliefs and attitudes. We've discussed how important these things are to being able to tap into the "spiritual you" and attract what you want. If you think you are not deserving of good things, then you hold yourself back.

You need to accept yourself and be willing to forgive yourself for any mistakes you've made in the past. Nobody is perfect; nobody goes through life without making any mistakes. It is too bad that we aren't just born with self-love. It would be a lot easier, but we have to develop it and decide to make it grow within us.

We need to respect the fact that we are spiritual beings and treat ourselves as if we are a powerful person who can succeed in anything we choose to do. Unfortunately, we are not born loving ourselves; we have to create that love. We can make our lives full of happiness and good things, or we can choose to be miserable and have a painful life. In the past I acted as if I were a victim because of what other people said and did or didn't do, as in the case of my father. I had to get past my self-made obstacles and choose to use the power in the "spiritual me." I learned to see the possibilities available to me because of that power.

I had to learn to accept myself and my past mistakes. Taking responsibility for myself was also part of the process of learning self-love. Then I needed to look at who I was becoming on this new path. I realized that I was changing and growing into a more powerful and loving person.

Remember that tapping into your thoughts and using them as tools will create strong feelings. I had to learn how to read my own feelings and not give in to the negative ones, but I also figured out that my feelings could help me break down certain obstacles. That was new for me. I realized that I needed to respect my feelings and then consciously respond to them in a constructive way. In the past I was very destructive, abusing drugs and alcohol and always running away from my problems.

"If we will just open ourselves to receive, like flowers opening to the sun, then everything is possible."

– Ti Caine

When you think about it, the universe is actually made up of love. If we think we're without love, then we haven't been aware of the world or the universe around us. If everything is literally made up of love, then we just need to open up to it. We must allow ourselves to take a bath in it and create a loving world for ourselves. Then we can share it with others who don't understand that love is always there for the receiving.

Part of loving yourself is to *not* settle for whatever is going on in your life without ever dreaming what it could be and then creating what you want. We have to stop blaming our past, what people have done to us, or what gifts we think God hasn't shared with us. We spend too much of our energy thinking we can't be any better than we are today and that life will just drag on until it's over. For a long time, I didn't want to believe that I created my own reality. As I started down this path I'm on, I learned to trust myself and love myself more so I could create a better life. Psychologists recognize that we have the power, through our thoughts, to create our own reality.

If we let ourselves just drift along on chance, we give up our inner power. This can cause us to feel helpless and depressed. We might not be able to control the challenges that come our way, but we can control our attitudes and reactions as we meet them.

I've always wanted to help other people get out of the holes we dig for ourselves. We can do so by lovingly helping others to recognize that we have the power to create something better and healthier, even from our failures. We have to be willing to look at ourselves and love who we see.

Stop for a minute and think about how you look at your past. Does it look like a junkyard full of stuff? Those are the problems and obstacles you've allowed to control you. They don't have to control you now or in your future. Love yourself. Forgive yourself. Accept that you are a spiritual being with power. This will give you the freedom to move forward in life, to use your inner power to create the success you want, and to be happy.

If you don't forgive yourself, you can't love yourself. This is something you have to work on from the inside out. The dictionary says that forgiveness means to pardon or excuse an action or a person. Be your own judge and pardon yourself. Then, forget it. Don't dwell on the negative, or you will attract the same thing back to you. Move on. Take responsibility for your choices, but don't spend hours beating yourself up over them. Recognize it, forgive it, and move forward to create what you want to be.

"You have many choices. You can choose forgiveness over revenge, joy over despair. You can choose action over apathy. You hold the key."

– Stephanie Marston

I have already talked about how I grew up thinking that I wasn't accepted or loved. Along my path, I've also learned that I chose limitations. For years, I thought I was helpless to change anything and just kept digging the hole I was in deeper and deeper. Things grew darker and darker. When I couldn't find acceptance in my family, I looked for it anywhere I could get it. Have you ever noticed that when children are not getting attention for good behavior, they will try to get it by doing something wrong? Parents will always respond to the bait of correcting a child when he or she is wrong. Think of the lesson parents teach this way.

We may not consciously think, "If I am doing something to get into trouble, I get attention, so I won't do anything *but* get into trouble." I think it is more of a subconscious thing; but remember, the conscious feeds thoughts to the subconscious and that creates physical action. I found acceptance from the "bad children" at school and chose to be one of them. We stuck together and kept doing drugs and alcohol. I'm sure, looking back, that some of them never got out of their rut and either died or went to prison for life. It could have been me if I hadn't chosen to make changes on having a different life than the one I had created for myself when I was younger.

Now that we've looked at where we've been, take a deep breath and imagine yourself in the future. See yourself being forgiven of your past. See what you look like and how you act as a more enlightened person. Visualize all the things you are and feel the acceptance. This will free you to create acceptance from others as well. You will see yourself getting the attention and love you need and attracting people into your life who will give you those things.

Loving yourself is not tied to what you do. It is accepting that you exist, that you are a creation of God and, therefore, do not have to prove your worth to anyone. Give yourself the opportunity to be who you are; think about the possibilities. You aren't defined by what other people think or say about you. Create a warm, caring, and concerned life for yourself with a healthy self-esteem and a feeling of value.

When you have moved on to this depth of self-love, you will find that you have created a much freer life for yourself. I learned I had something to offer other people to help them overcome obstacles and create better lives for themselves. I could use my experiences to help other people because I have been where they are. I didn't have to hide behind a self-made mask so that people wouldn't know who the real me was. I didn't have to be controlled by trying to please others. It was great to feel like the chains of my self-made prison were finally unlocked. I realized I was completely responsible for my own feelings and actions. No one controls them but me.

I hope this chapter has helped you to understand what healthy self-love is and how important it is for building the stepping stones on the path to success. Let's look at moving that circle out to loving others. You can take all the same principles we've talked about and apply them to your family, your friends, business acquaintances, and people you attract and who may help you realize your dreams.

Loving others isn't just about physical attraction. It is about accepting them for all that they are and cherishing them for being what they are with you. It includes their past mistakes and history, their attitudes, and how they act. There have been many books written about practicing tough love. It's loving others in spite of their "warts" and helping them to become better people - even when it is difficult, even when they do bad things.

Choose to attract lovable people into your life. Look for the qualities that you admire or want to emulate. You also have to be the person you want to love. It will cause a vibration in you that is like a tuning fork. If you hit a tuning fork on a table in the same room with a piano, the same note will vibrate in the piano. People are like that. If we are positive and creative, we attract positive and creative people into our lives. If we are loving and accepting we will get loving and accepting people in our lives.

You may ask: "What about my ex-husband or ex-wife?" Stop and think of where you were then. Were you negative? Did you expect life to just keep giving you junk? Were you willing to settle for whatever came along? Were you afraid nothing better would come to you, so you attracted whatever was out there? Your state of mind and self-love attracts the people who vibrate to the same note. It works just like the tuning fork.

After you've made the changes in yourself like I did when I went through the process of telling myself "I love you," the next step is to start believing it and acting like it. It is how I attracted my wife, Janet, into my life. It's not that Teresa, my first wife, was a bad person; it's just that we were both in a bad place back then, so we attracted each other. We didn't help each other create a better life together because we didn't really know how. As we both grew, we grew apart. We weren't good for each other.

The concept of treating other people the way you want to be treated is a good way to be in a friendship, business relationship, or personal relationship. Christians call it "The Golden Rule." Be accepting of others and realize that they have the same kind of spiritual power that you do, whether they know it or not. Everyone you meet has value and wants acceptance. When you can accept that you are okay just the way you are, you can then accept others for being the way they are.

Sometimes it's hard to open yourself up to someone else. It's risky. You have experienced rejection before and don't want to go through it again. Most of my life, I suffered from what I felt was my father's rejection. Then I learned I didn't have to do that anymore.

"You need to be aware of what others are doing, applaud their efforts, acknowledge their successes, and encourage them in their pursuits. When we all help one another, everybody wins."

– Jim Stovall

We attract others into our lives with the same vibrations that we have. Our spiritual self has a field of natural vibrations that is tied to our minds and our thoughts. When I look back, I must admit that my spiritual side gave me some very valuable lessons. Because of my living conditions in Arizona, I went looking for a job. That was how I met Kim and the other guys at the lumberyard, and meeting them started me on a spiritual path that I'm still on today.

You are responsible for choosing to attract positive and loving people to you, but when you're wandering around in a fog and can't figure out which way is up, the universe will bring certain things and people into your circle. I can choose to connect or not. I connected with the guys at the lumberyard because I learned they had stories like mine. We attracted each other without my consciously knowing it at the time. Once you know how the Law of Attraction works, you can consciously make it work for you.

Like the acceptance you have for yourself, when you are around other people who are supportive, you can always be yourself. You don't have to be afraid of their getting back at you for something you said or did. You are consciously choosing to be a better person, and they are letting you know that they love you as you are.

After you've attracted someone into your life, think about how relationships grow. Relationships develop through a bonding process. Your positive energy and feelings are a big part of it. The dictionary says that bonding is "the physical and emotional phenomenon between individuals and the others in their environment." More importantly, bonding is necessary for the development of a healthy self-esteem.

When you apply the things we've discussed about self-love, you can feel a sense of security and safety with another person. This works with friends, children, family, spouses, and others. You start giving unconditional love to each other because you accept them and they accept you. You're not just doing things that they want you to do, you're continuing to be yourself. At first, it is in your thoughts, then in your feelings, and ultimately in your actions.

You can see yourself doing things with that person that you both enjoy. You have plans that include them in your dreams for the future. When you become close, you can have shared dreams and goals that you help each other to realize. You don't have to give up being you to be with the other person. As you progress and grow separately, you also become closer in your relationship. You encourage each other in all aspects of your life. You want each other to be self-confident and be positive.

When you are getting closer to someone, your positive energy will be accepting and help you cope with obstacles. That makes you stronger both when you are together and when you are apart. If the other person in your relationship is detached and rejects your ideas and you, then obviously this relationship should not be maintained. Let it go. If one of you is quick to blame the other for things, or if you condemn each other for what you did in the past, that is a bad relationship to be in. Choose to be in one that has a spirit of cooperation, helpfulness, understanding, and forgiveness. Together, you will attract a better life that you can share.

Let's widen our circle. Move on to helping others around you in your neighborhood, your city, your state, or even nationally. Maybe even the world. It can grow as big as you want to dream. Be a caring and loving person to others.

It's also important to avoid flaunting what you've learned. Have you ever watched someone who learned something valuable and within five minutes lecture others about this knowledge? Most of us experience that as arrogance. It is a mistake to act as though you already "have it all together" when you've only started on your path. Most of us struggle with keeping it together all the time, and we all suffer moments of setback and failure. Maintain some humility as you succeed, and more people will be drawn to your message.

With a positive outlook and by attracting positive relationships into our circle, we can make a difference in how our whole world is. It is a difference made one person at a time with the support and encouragement of ourselves and others.

We are all somewhere on a path to success, and we can help each other find a better way. It's not always the easiest or shortest path, but it is the one on which you will grow and realize that you have it within your power to make things happen. If someone you know is still suffering through problems that seem to overwhelm them, be supportive and encourage them to find their inner spirit. You may be the one having a hard time, so use the tools we are talking about to tap into your inner spirit and use that power to be what you really want to be. And let others help you.

When you look at your obstacles, remember that the universe is made of love. Choose to see it that way. It will make the obstacles easier to push through. Visualize yourself loved and successful. The universe will provide you with the details. Take the steps you know how to take first and, believe me, the other things you need to do to build the rest of the path will come to you when you need them.

Do you ever wonder how you just happen to meet the right person at the right time, or read a self-help book that told you what you needed right then? It's the Law of Attraction at work in your life. Use it. It's your power to use with the real you.

Over time and with practice at loving yourself and others, tapping into the love of the universe will become easier. You will become a better problem solver, and you will see yourself that way. Your world is full of options and alternatives to help you face problems at home, school, work, or in your neighborhood. It can extend to solving world problems, too. It starts with you and how you think and how you love.

"Love is the ability and willingness to allow those that you care for to be what they choose for themselves without any insistence that they satisfy you."

– Wayne Dyer

Since we don't want others to expect us to live the life they want for us, then we need to remember not to push our dreams and intentions on others. Their dreams may be different from yours, but you can love them unconditionally by letting them realize their own dreams. It goes back to mutual respect for each other's feelings and thoughts. When our paths cross, we can enjoy each other's support. Be willing to support your children and friends in their dreams, just as you expect them to support you in yours.

Otherwise, you go backwards. You will get caught in that old trap called resentment because someone else didn't do what you wanted them to do. It's better if you don't go back to that one; it hurts you and your relationship with others. Part of loving others is to let go and let them experience life as they see it. If the life you see yourself in is the same life as someone else, then you will get to experience the joy of doing it together.

I had to realize that love is a verb; it's not a noun or adjective. That means I need to do it for myself first and then share it with others. Have you ever noticed that the more love and respect you have for yourself, the more you have to share? Love is something that, when you share it, you get back more than you sent out. It is part of what vibrates in the real you. You can surround yourself with the love that is already out there in the universe. You just need to begin with yourself and grow it outwards. Try it. You'll be amazed at how abundant your life will become.

PERSONAL COACHING ACTIVITY

You're going to share my experience of taking those first steps to love yourself. I'm asking you to do what my counselor asked me to do. It is important to develop the love of self, so you can love others.

1. Look at yourself in the mirror each morning and evening and say, "I love you." Be sure to actually make eye contact with yourself as you do it. Repeat this for the next seven days.

2. At the end of the seven days, journal about your experience. How did you feel the first time? How do you feel now?

3. Keep saying "I love you" to your reflection each morning and evening for the next 14 days. Write out your feelings and how they have changed and how your experience has progressed. Let me assure you that healthy self-love is a foundational step that makes a huge difference.

CHAPTER

So, Now What Do I Do?

"Learning keeps one from being led astray."

– Chinese Proverb

We've gone through some theories, and I've shared some of my experiences with you. I've read many books and attended seminars that gave me great information, but some of them left me without knowing how to actually apply the concepts in my daily life. I felt frustrated. I hope to give you some assistance in moving our discussions and exercises into enlightenment and enlargement in your life. Realize that we all need other people to help us along our path. At this point in your journey, I want to be that person.

> *"Desire is the key to motivation, but it's determination and commitment to an unrelenting pursuit of your goal — a commitment to excellence — that will enable you to attain the success you seek."*
>
> **– Mario Andretti**

One concept you should be able to take with you is that nothing is impossible. No matter where you are on the status ladder, you can overcome anything. Together we've learned how to develop awareness of ourselves, breathe through our challenges, move toward a better self-image, find our dreams, and know that we are spiritual beings with endless creativity and possibilities. We've discussed some of the changes that will take place in your life when you adopt an attitude of gratitude. Another stepping stone is belief in ourselves. Believe and prepare to be amazed. Have faith in yourself. You also need to adopt the habit of never giving up on what you want. It's okay if you fall a few times on the way; just get up and keep going. You don't fail unless you quit. The people who succeed in life are the ones that persist. And above all, don't forget that love is the foundation for everything in life. First you learn to love and respect yourself, then you learn to love and respect those around you.

My mission and purpose in life is to be committed to what I love. My true passion is experiencing the feeling I get when I'm helping bring awareness to those who want to unlock their gifts and potential within them.

I believe that the fundamental nature of life is uncomplicated. We as humans are programmed to make things hard for ourselves. The miracle of life is discovering the true essence of who we really are. We can learn to become a person we can truly love. My desire is to show you how to uncover your gifts in a way that gives you a map to follow. I've learned many lessons, both in spite of and because of the obstacles I've overcome in my life. It took me years to find peace for myself. I want to help each of you reach a place of peace in a world of chaos, and to find it faster than I did.

The first major obstacle we talked about was my behavior toward my family and my school. Over the years, I have come to terms with my relationship with my parents. My parents lived in Washington state for most of their lives. Mother passed away in 1995 from heart problems. My father passed away in July of 2004 from ALS. They had worked in their bakery, The Cake Box, in Kent, Washington, for over 30 years. My two brothers and my sister are still alive. I had to change how I viewed our relationships, how they affected my life, and what part of that I chose to create. Now that I know we can choose how we will continue our lives, even if we can't change our past, I have turned my resentment into contentment.

While I was in school, I must say I did a great job living up to the labels they gave me: "troublemaker" and "stupid." I made a habit of living down to their expectations until I learned how to break out of my old habits. Now, years later and after much personal growth, I love humor and making people laugh. I enjoy having a good time with others.

Early in learning how to change my life into what I wanted, I spent a lot of time drifting and feeling like I was out of control. As I recall that place in my life now, I realize that my experience was kind of like vertigo. Everyone has had a dizzy spell at one time or another. Some people get disoriented when they look down from high places. Vertigo is the feeling that you or the objects around you are whirling around in space. It can be a symptom of some physical condition or disease. The feeling of spinning is actually from an imbalance or disturbance in the inner ear. In the grip of vertigo, you literally don't know which way is up.

Years ago I worked up on Mount Bachelor cleaning the lodges. One of the lodges I cleaned was called Pine Martin. The only way to get up there was to ride the chair lift. After I got off work, the lift wasn't running, and I would have to call the slope groomers to come and pick me up.

One night, we were having white-out conditions. You couldn't see anything. There were six groomers and me, and we all needed to get down the mountain. We went together with the most experienced driver in front because he knew the mountain better than anyone else. As we were coming down the slopes, I felt strange. I couldn't tell which way was up or down. I didn't know if we were on our side or flipped over backwards. It was the strangest experience I'd ever had. That was the first time I experienced vertigo in the physical sense.

I think our lives can be a lot like vertigo. We feel off-balance and don't know what direction to go. We feel completely out of our element.

Another way to look at it is like a fish out of water. They flop around until they die if you put them on dry land. Someone has to come along and rescue them by putting them back in the water.

I've had several businesses of my own over the years. When I sold my yard maintenance business, I felt like it took away my true north. I was used to the daily and seasonal routine of it, and I found it hard to accept the change in my life. Nevertheless, it was an adjustment that gave me a chance to spend some time looking at and questioning the direction of my life.

Many times, our ego gets in the way of our better judgment. We forget that we are a soul experiencing physical circumstances. We have a higher power, a God force that lives in us, around us, and gives us the spirit that we truly are, but we have the power to ignore it as well as to listen to it.

"Vertigo is not a comfortable place for your personality, which likes things to be certain and secure. Vertigo is a time when you are learning to think in new ways. If you are experiencing vertigo in any area of your life, love yourself, do not worry if no direction has yet revealed itself."

– Sanaya Roman

Remember that you can tap into your spiritual self through engaging in daily prayer and meditation, going to church, or communing with nature. Such things restore our perspective and bring us back into balance.

My other obstacles grew out of low self-esteem, a poor self-image, and wanting to escape my reality. I thought that traveling, drugs, and alcohol were the answer, but they just gave me more problems to overcome. It was hard, but how different my life is now compared to when I was young. At that time, I had never thought there was anything but what I surrounded myself with. I made my problems larger than they were originally through my thoughts, my attitudes, and the actions that resulted from them.

If we learn to develop our true power and potential, we can change our lives and help others change theirs. Our self-image is how we see ourselves, but it influences how we see the rest of the world, as well. I learned that the mind is our "true-self," or spirit, and that it is part of our thought center.

How superficial are you? Most of us focus on the "wrapper," that is, the way we appear on the outside. Wayne Dyer gives an example to explain this concept. He says that it's like going to the grocery store and buying broccoli or almonds. They come in a sealed wrapper. Before putting them into the microwave oven at home, we tear off the package; instead of putting the vegetable in to cook, we put the plastic wrap in. We are so focused on the outside that we forget the real food is on the inside of the package.

Most of us hold an image of ourselves that only comes from the outside. I used to reason that I did what I did because of the way I was raised. It was because of the economy that I was beaten and neglected. I didn't get a fair shake after the new boss came to work. It was his fault. This type of defeatist thinking can go on and on.

Earl Nightingale put together a tape series called *The Greatest Secret*. He said the secret was that we become what we think about all day. If that's true, what do you think about? Are your thoughts consumed with the bills or the abundance around you that is available? We can waste our time thinking about scarcity and a lack of things we want, or we can spend our time expecting abundance. Sometimes it's just a matter of putting on your glasses and really seeing the possibilities.

When you think about your job, you have the choice to hate it or to be open to the possibilities within you for a different career.

*"Choose a job you love, and you will never
have to work a day in your life."*

– Confucius

You can sit there on your couch wondering why your life hasn't amounted to a hill of beans, or you can consider what options there are. Take responsibility for choosing to let things happen to you instead of focusing on what you want your life to be. Don't just let things happen to you, make them happen around you.

*"Some people make things happen, some
people watch things happen, and some
people wonder what happened."*

– Don Warrick

I often hear people complain about their jobs, saying they don't think they are getting paid enough for what demands are put on them by their employers. If you're worth more than that, decide to do what it takes to have a career that pays you what you are really worth. Don't settle for whatever comes along. Focus on the amount you want to make, what you want to do, and attract those things into your circle.

How many times do you or your friends say you wish you could go on a vacation, and then never go anywhere? Watch the Travel Channel and decide where you want to go. Make it happen. Don't be stuck in the mind-set of always being focused on all the things you'll never have or see. You've trapped yourself back in the box we talked about in the first chapter of this book.

Think about the house or apartment where you and your family live right now. That building started with a thought. Then it became a blueprint for the builder. All the steps were taken to make the drawing and the blueprint become a physical form.

Our lives are that way. The problem is that we don't plan it out in detail like someone building a house or a skyscraper. We each have a blueprint inside of us that was put there before we were born. Genetic conditioning and environmental factors influence what happens to us as we grow to adulthood. Whether they are positive or negative conditionings, we carry those blueprints with us and keep looking at them. My purpose in this book is to help you overcome that blueprint, so you can make a conscious decision to change the way you think. Each chapter has taken you through some activities to lay a foundation for your changes. I want you to try those exercises, and I want to help you apply them so you can create the abundant life you want.

The activities are meant to build on one another. In the first chapter, we worked on becoming aware of yourself and your potential. Self-reflection is where you have to make the changes you want. You examined the beliefs that you hold about yourself and made a list. Then you thought about where those beliefs came from, and I asked you to just look at them as if they belonged to someone else.

You need to know what you believe about yourself. You have old tapes running in your mind that affects your present and future. Remember, you need not get emotional about them; just know that they are there and they have affected your life. You only want to hold on to the beliefs and thoughts about yourself that are good and true. All the others can be erased.

Next, in Chapter 2 we talked about breathing and how it is related to the inner you – your spirit. We talked about how fear can be an obstacle unless we realize that it's usually an irrational and emotional reaction to something that is unknown to us. The activities were centered on two lists. You were to write your biggest problems. Then you were to journal about how they made you feel. If you haven't done the coaching activities yet, you may want to go back and do them now. You will get more from the information in this book if you take an active part and begin the process of changing your life. Thoughts and dreams should result in a change of your mind frame and your actions. The great thing about journaling your feelings and reactions is that it is a healthy way to express frustrations and anger, as well as to get things out where you can see them. Don't forget to brainstorm for solutions, and talk to your mentor or supportive friends.

In Chapter 3, we concentrated on self-image – where it comes from and how to develop a new and better one. You made a list of positive things about yourself and then a negative list that you could destroy. The act of destroying the negative list is a demonstration of how you can intentionally get rid of negatives in your life. I hope you will follow the directions and make index cards with positive affirmations about yourself. Repeat them until they become habits and ingrained in your thinking patterns. It is an important part of the process. The more positive you are, the more you will attract positive people and experiences.

Chapter 4 encourages you to find out what your dreams and passions are. This one should be a lot of fun. Don't forget to dream BIG. If it takes you awhile to make a list of your interests, just keep a running list on a notepad until you are finished. Don't limit yourself to a few that quickly come to mind. Keep going deeper until there isn't anything else. Keep asking yourself, "What else?" Focus on your top three as suggested in the coaching activities. That doesn't mean you should give up on the others because they can come later, or as a result of accomplishing the others. Really concentrate one the first one that is most important. You may add to your dreams as you go through life, which is perfectly fine; we all change the things we want from time to time. So, it's okay to want what you want.

The first four coaching activities are meant to help you sort out your thoughts and feelings in order to discover what you really want in life. They give you the first steps in building the new you. You have to know about yourself in order to know what to change. This will shake up your thought processes so you can become who you can be. From your passion comes your purpose. Like I've said, mine is helping others, but yours may be different. What is important, though, is that you find your purpose, your dream, and pursue it!

Chapter 5 teaches that we are not just physical beings; we are actually spiritual beings here for experiences. Some readers may not have heard this concept before or not realized that you aren't confined by the shell you live in. I've been a lot of things – a son, student, brother, husband, provider, protector, father, friend, landscaper, baker, and minister. But those labels aren't the real me.

The real me, who I truly am, is the spiritual part of me that is connected to my Creator. The spiritual essence inside of me is made up of love, kindness, happiness, joy, freedom, forgiveness, grace, and compassion.

We all have those qualities, but at the same time we are distinct individuals. God created me in his likeness and image but only made one unique Dean with my eyes, hair, skin tone, fingerprints, and DNA. Each of us has an inner connection that is particular only to us because of God's love.

That is the "you" we are working to let out, so you express the power inside you. It is there for you to use. So why not realize your full potential? The journaling activities for this chapter are meant to help you key in on the difference between using negative and positive energy, which will feel good and attract good things to you. Teach yourself to consciously make the effort to surround yourself with internal and external positive energy and people. They will encourage you and help you realize your spirituality.

Take the tools out of your toolbox that we reviewed. The six intellectual factors — perception, will, memory, intuition, imagination, and reason — unlock your ability to tap into the spiritual power you possess.

The choices we talked about in Chapter 6 are concrete. Remember that you can either let life happen to you, or you can be proactive and be the one making the decision. One thing that makes us wealthy and allows us to realize the abundance around us is the idea that we have many choices. The more choices you have, the richer you are. Trusting yourself is important. Take a chance. You've taken chances trusting others, so you can trust yourself. Look at all the great things you've learned about yourself, and appreciate yourself for the person you are.

Surround yourself with supportive people and positive experiences. If something happens that you don't experience as positive, figure out what lesson you can learn from it and be glad for the lesson. When you make the list of changes you want to make, don't limit yourself. Your spirit is not limited; don't restrict yourself to little things. Once again, think outside the box.

Actively look for someone to be your mentor and find an accountability partner, so you can share your victories and challenges with him or her. You can help each other to reach your goals. It is important to remember not to do this alone because we need each other on this journey.

The attitude of gratitude in Chapter 7 makes a huge difference. Attitude can make you or break you. Sometimes, when we make choices that don't turn out as we had hoped, our attitude is what gets us through. We can be thankful in all things. It doesn't mean we have to be perfectly happy about everything, but we can find the good in it and be thankful for that. In the coaching activities, you made a list of those things you are thankful for. The list may change from day to day, and it should. You might be thankful today that the 12 inches of snow you were supposed to get last night turned out to be only five inches, and you were able to drive to a seminar you wanted to attend. It still snowed, but it's much easier. The passes are probably still open if you live near the mountains. If you live in a flat area, you could be thankful it didn't drift and you can still drive down the road. I'm not saying to be fake and cheery about everything; be realistic, but don't concentrate on the negative side of every experience.

The really fun part of these exercises is the list of what you want to attract to you in the next six months. Learn to be grateful for what you have now and what you will have in the future.

Chapter 8 asks you to believe. It is important for you to believe in yourself and your dreams. Have faith that they will come true. See yourself receiving the life you are meant to have. Moreover, belief is a "heart issue." Your belief ties into your emotions and inner self, creating energy and attracting the life you want to you.

The coaching activities are almost like the game you probably played as a child, make-believe. The exception now is that it's not just pretend anymore. It is visualizing yourself and how it will feel to have the cabin by the lake. The second part is to look back at your list of attributes. You may still be struggling with these. Tie it into your beliefs. See yourself as those things because you really are those things. Your spirit knows it.

In Chapter 9 we talked about the difference that persistence makes. We are focusing on your success in the coaching activities. You have all the stepping stones to get to this point if you actively use the process we've been through so far. Persisting seems like a simple thing, but too many times we forget to do that. It's like breathing. Don't stop.

You're going to get resistance from people around you. Sometimes the most resistance will come from the people to whom you are the closest, but remember that *no* is just a word. It only stops you from succeeding if you believe it. Your beliefs about yourself and what you can have in this life are changing. It isn't instant; part of persistence is being patient with yourself and others.

If you are working with other people to get what you want out of life, the load is easier to carry. Don't fall back into the trap of thinking you have to do everything if anything is to get done. Stay positive.

To me, one of the fun things of believing you are a good person and helpful to others, that you can make a difference in your life, is the overwhelming positive energy that builds on itself. You attract more positive people to you, and that makes it easier to keep going.

Don't forget the second part of the coaching exercises, which is to write out a plan. It doesn't have to be complicated and 30 pages long with every detail. The universe will take care of some of the details for you. It can be one page of your ideas. Then, focus on the results you expect. Visualize them. Those positive thoughts will let you know what the action steps are for your plan. Trust yourself. Trust those around you who are helping you on your path. A trip is always more fun if you're not by yourself.

Finally, we talked about the effect of love in my life and yours. First, I had to learn to love myself and then love others. You have to face your *stuff* when you learn to love yourself again, but it is really worth the trouble to go through it. It is painful sometimes, but you can be grateful for the process and the change that will come in your life when you allow love to be a big part of it. In 2000, I met a beautiful woman, Janet, who has made a huge difference in my life. At the time, I wasn't even looking for and didn't really want a relationship.

If I hadn't gone through the process of changing myself - my attitudes and expectations - and becoming a positive person, I probably would have missed the possibility of having a great relationship with my wife, Janet. We've grown together and separately. The best part of our growth together is our family. We have five wonderful daughters, Heather, Heidi, Kristina, Jeannette, and Amber. WOW! It can be interesting sometimes. We currently have three grandchildren and one on the way. Our family is growing.

Learn to let go of resentment and anger with yourself and others; otherwise, it will only poison you. You're the one that suffers the most. Keep reminding yourself that a healthy self-love, not just ego, is a good thing. When you decide to do something, you've made an agreement with yourself, and it needs to be kept just like you keep them with other people. That doesn't mean you're stuck with it if you need to make a change in your life. It only affects your self-esteem when you break an agreement. If you renegotiate it with yourself or others, it isn't broken. It is changed in a healthy way.

I hope you did the "I love you" exercise, no matter what it made you feel like at first. I shared with you how I went through the same process when my counselor told me I needed to love myself. If you haven't started it yet, now is a good time to do that. Keep in mind that if you pick and choose which stepping stones you use, your path will have gaps in it, and you will probably trip over the uneven ground. Unfortunately, that is something that I learned the hard way.

Most people don't journal because they think it is like keeping a diary. Maybe it reminds us men of when we were children and our sisters kept that little pink diary with the silver key in the drawer by her bed and wrote down all kinds of stuff about the boys she liked. You may have stolen it when she was gone and read parts of it. Keeping a diary may have seemed stupid to you at the time. Journaling is different. It is not a recap of what you did today. It doesn't even have to be daily.

Unlike a daily diary, journaling can help you through the process. Just go to a store and get a cheap spiral notebook in the school supply section. Write in it what you think and how you feel about things. You can even use it as a way to vent your frustrations and record your successes. You never have to let anyone see it. (I wouldn't leave it laying around where others can accidentally come across it.) Journaling is a really good way to figure out how you feel. It can help you sort things out for yourself. It gets rid of the negative stuff, and lets you move on to the positive feelings and thoughts. It's a good tool for getting things turned around in your life, so you can attract the people and things you want.

"Success means having the courage, the determination, and the will to become the person you believe you were meant to be."

– George Sheehan

You are what you think about most of the time. I had learned to take responsibility for that in my life. I had to stop blaming everyone else for my problems. We have the power in us to be whatever we really want to be. Since everything you've done up to now makes you who you are and is why you have what you have, it makes sense that what your dreams for the future can also be produced by what you do today and tomorrow.

I encourage you to feel your fears, but just do the things you need to anyway, in spite of your fears. After awhile, your comfort zone will be larger, and what felt scary before won't be an obstacle to you anymore. Go to the bookstore or library and read positive books, self-help books, and anything that helps you along your path. Go to seminars like the ones I do; mine or others who will teach you the tools you need. Then surround yourself with positive and supportive people. Also, be able to accept where you are on your path and know that it takes a while to get where you're going.

The Buddha said that life was not just for destinations, but for the journey. The experiences you have, both positive and negative, will make you the wonderful person you are. Enjoy each one of the steps on your way. Some are harder than others, but be glad you are progressing toward your dreams.

Don't waste your time just wishing and hoping in your feelings of fear. Some say the biggest obstacle to being successful is our own fear of failure. We focus on lack and doubt and end up never taking the first step. Then, we hang around in the *Misery Zone* and wonder why our lives are so bad. Truly positive thoughts end up in actions. Every action may not be the right one, but in the end, as long as you stay focused on the dream and the successful results you want, you haven't changed directions.

Take a look in the mirror. That person you see may not be recognizable, but it's you. Who you are is who you've created. If you don't like it, then start with the first stepping stone and work through the chapters. It really is worth the effort. Some people say that the eyes are a window to the soul. Have you ever noticed that negative and unhappy people seem to have dull eyes? I'm not talking about when you have the flu and your eyes look tired; I'm talking about every day. Other people have a glow about them, and their eyes shine. Those are the people you want to hang out with and become friends with.

Decide you want the person in the mirror to be the one you want to be. All the potential is wrapped up in your spirit. Your spirit will endure long after your physical body is gone. It is literally the definition of persistence and your future. The "wrapping" you see around it is just that, the outside. The good stuff is inside, like a birthday present, so open it up and enjoy yourself.

I've found that the best thing in life is to do what you love, not just make a living to pay the bills. If you've been through all the coaching activities, you are changing your attitude which means you're changing your life and your future.

The longer I have spent on this path of enlightenment and the more aware I am of the Law of Attraction, the more joyous things I attract to myself. I attracted Paul Martinelli and Bob Proctor and their guidance, which has been huge. They are helping point me in the direction of my dreams, and they're giving me the tools to make them happen. That's what I am sharing with you.

The more you love and respect yourself and are aware of the Law of Attraction, the more you will realize the world is your playground. No toy is too big or too much money for you to have. The greatest thing I've learned is that I can have anything I want. I attract things, and life is fun. You can enjoy everything you are blessed with. The Law of Attraction is real – in my life and in yours.

Nelson Mandela used a quote from Maryanne Williamson in his 1994 inaugural speech in South Africa. It is a good guide for us to use in overcoming that obstacle of fear that sometimes pops up when we think we have things under control.

"Our deepest fear is not that we are inadequate. Our deepest fear is that we are powerful beyond measure. It is our light, not our darkness, that frightens us most. We ask ourselves, 'Who am I to be brilliant, gorgeous, talented, and famous?' Actually, who are you not to be? You are a child of God. Your 'playing small' does not serve the world. There is nothing enlightened about shrinking so that people won't feel insecure around you. We were born to make manifest the glory of God that is within us. It's not just in some of us; it's in all of us. And when we let our own light shine, we unconsciously give other people permission to do the same. As we are liberated from our own fear, our presence automatically liberates others."

To put it in other words, nothing changes until point of view changes. This truth is one of the main things I've learned and want to pass on to you. If we keep doing the same old thing we've always done, then we can expect to get the same results. Nothing will change. The stepping stones we've gone through on this part of our journey together can be that change in your point of view.

The biggest problem with our viewpoint is that we only see us from inside. We don't have the advantage of being in someone else's mind or experience. The awareness, breathing, and spiritual exercises will help you get outside of yourself a little. That's what we must do; we must look at ourselves as others see us to give us a clearer picture of ourselves. Sometimes we are too close to our own problems to see them. If you have others around you for support, they can help you see what you can't see by yourself.

When you are exchanging thoughts and encouragement with each other, it needs to be helpful and build you up, not tear you down. Helping each other is what it is about. We change ourselves and the world one person at a time. Concentrate on the things you see that you like and that are positive. If you are going to address something that is negative, it needs to be done in a loving way. Tell others what they are doing well and what needs more focus. Praise the things those around you do well. People react better to praise. It goes back to expectations for yourself and others. But never praise what you do not admire. At those times, it is better to be honest.

Most of all, I encourage you to be all that you can. Tap into the real you in your spirit. We've traveled together for a little while. Remember to love yourself and dream big. Stay committed to unlocking your self-made prison. Use your imagination and create the things you want to come into your reality. Use the Law of Attraction for your benefit. The world is a smorgasbord, just waiting for you to indulge yourself.

Go. Feast. Live.

Dean Storer
LifeSuccess Consultant

In life, we are sometimes scared or unsure of how to move forward. We have been taught to often too put away our own dreams to focus on "the real world." My desire is to show you how to bring your dreams to life. I coach individuals and companies coaching them on how to be, do, and have what they desire and give seminars on the products and information that you will fall in love with in this book. My personal desire is to show people how to live up to their unlimited possibilities and unlock the uniqueness we all have within us. I would love the opportunity to show you how you can have a fuller richer life or company. What I am offering benefits all. Think about your staff: if they were happier, wouldn't they produce more for your company? If you were happier, wouldn't everything in your life move at a smoother pace? Let me help make it happen for you!

GET THE RESULTS YOU WANT
CALL TODAY!

Dean Storer
541-390-5948   or email
deanstorer@LifeSuccessConsultants.com

PRODUCTS FROM OUR LifeSuccess Library!

This is the seminar program to master the skills and life-changing concepts we teach. Everything is broken down and delivered by my mentor, Bob Proctor, in front of an audience and a chalkboard, and is backed up by DVDs and CDs to reinforce the material. In this program, you will unlock the hidden and rich potential that allows you to achieve every financial, emotional, physical, and spiritual dream you have imagined for yourself.

- How your mind works
- What The Comfort Zone is and how to break out of it
- The most effective method for tapping into – and changing – your powerful subconscious conditioning
- The simple Formula for Financial Freedom
- How to utilize the universal Creative Process to your great advantage
- Implementing the Razor's Edge formula to win

$697.99 U.S. available online at

www.deanstorer.LifeSuccessconsultants.com

The ultimate tool for any commissioned salesperson or those working in a service industry. With simple step-by-step instructions, Bob Proctor takes you to a 6- or 7-figure income without you having to work any harder. As you get involved in this program, you will find yourself finally and forever stepping across the line that separates so many struggling salespeople from those who win big – month after month and year after year. You will learn the six basic concepts you MUST understand before you will ever learn large commissions, and the one fundamental step you must develop to earn $100,000+ while still enjoying your work.

Offers a thorough understanding of how each element of your being works to bring about the results you are currently getting in your life and to move towards what you truly desire. You will gain the power to transform your life into anything you choose by setting goals that you really want, prioritizing them, and then learning the focus and action skills to achieve one after another. You will learn how to repeat the process. This program will take you step by step directly towards any goal you truly desire.

$199.99 U.S. AVAILABLE ONLINE AT

WWW.DEANSTORER.LIFESUCCESSCONSULTANTS.COM

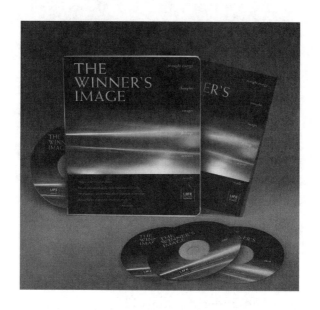

Your self-image is like the thermostat in your home – try to obtain success without adjusting your self-image, and it will bring you right back to where it has been "set" by others in the past. This program is key to building confidence in adults and teens alike. This is a strong action-oriented program with powerful emphasis on accountability. With THIS change, nothing will change in your life! The Winner's Image teaches you that you can shift and choose more beneficial power in your life by shifting how you perceive yourself first.

$199.99 U.S. AVAILABLE ONLINE AT

WWW.DEANSTORER.LIFESUCCESSCONSULTANTS.COM

Arranging for your own success is like putting a puzzle together. You use the picture on the box to know where the pieces go. Without a clear, defined picture of your success, you have no idea where the pieces of your life should go. This program develops that picture with your help. With this Success Puzzle Program, you'll be finding, recognizing, and putting in place every piece you need to create a much more successful life. You will learn how to eliminate all obstacles blocking the paths to your dreams and goals, and study and implement the most foundational pieces for your own success picture.

$199.99 U.S. AVAILABLE ONLINE AT

WWW.DEANSTORER.LIFESUCCESSCONSULTANTS.COM

The Science of Getting RICH CLUB®

Designed by The Teachers Featured in "The Secret"

Dr. Michael Beckwith   Bob Proctor   Jack Canfield

The Secret Behind "The Secret" Science of Getting Rich Home Study Course: $1,995.00 More Powerful than Any DVD, Book, Seminar, or Course!

Here's What You Will Get...

1. Never-Before-Recorded Audio Instruction

With this program, you will be one of the privileged few to gain access to never-before-recorded audio instruction and summaries of lessons and observations from the teachers, Bob Proctor and Jack Canfield. The 10 audio CDs are jam-packed with their tutelage.

2. Bob Proctor and Jack Canfield, always by your side.

We will also give you a compact digital MP3 player preloaded with 15 hours of content, which means you will be totally immersed in the program IMMEDIATELY and CONSTANTLY to ensure you effect the Law of Attraction to bring you wealth EVERYDAY!

Immerse yourself anytime and anywhere! Listen anytime while in a bus, on a train, waiting in line, during lunch breaks, by the pool ...

3. Tools to Help You Take Action and Keep It Going

Fifteen Dynamic Lessons that capture specific teachings to help you further understand and implement the Law of Attraction and other Universal Laws. Taught by Bob Proctor and summarized by Jack Canfield.

Compact Personal Vision Boards for mapping out and envisioning the life you seek to attract.

Multiple Sources of Income (MSI) Whiteboards that motivate and inspire you to create New Channels of Wealth.

A Science of Getting Rich Goal Card – one of the primary foundational pieces in the absolute realization of your dreams.

4. New Opportunities, a Support System, and Continuous Learning

$500 Gift Certificate to attend a live seminar worldwide to continue learning in a live seminar environment!

Instant global connections for all your networking and connection needs. These online, active communities, masterminds, blogs, and discussion boards welcome your participation and insights, as you grow through this tremendous process.

The Original Science of Getting Rich Book beautifully redesigned for this Briefcase, which means that ANYONE can master and internalize the wisdom of the ORIGINAL text without exception!

5. A Complete Training System in One Powerful Briefcase

A Rich, Supple Leather-Bound Briefcase specially designed to contain The Home Seminar Kit so that you can take it with you EVERYWHERE with no hassle. ALL THIS delivered to your doorstep.

ORDER YOUR BRIEFCASE TODAY AT:

WWW.DEANSTORER.LIFESUCCESSCONSULTANTS.COM

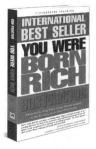

You Were Born Rich

Bob Proctor
ISBN # 978-0-9656264-1-5

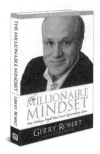

The Millionaire Mindset
*How Ordinary People Can
Create Extraordinary Income*

Gerry Robert
ISBN # 978-1-59930-030-6

Rekindle The Magic In
Your Relationship
Making Love Work

Anita Jackson
ISBN # 978-1-59930-041-2

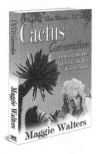

Finding The Bloom of
The Cactus Generation
*Improving the quality of
life for Seniors*

Maggie Walters
ISBN # 978-1-59930-011-5

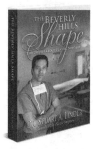

The Beverly Hills Shape
The Truth About Plastic Surgery

Dr. Stuart Linder
ISBN # 978-1-59930-049-8

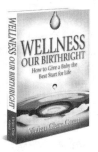

Wellness Our Birthright
*How to give a baby the best
start in life.*

Vivien Clere Green
ISBN # 978-1-59930-020-7

Lighten Your Load

Peter Field
ISBN # 978-1-59930-000-9

Change & How To
Survive In The New
Economy
*7 steps to finding freedom
& escaping the rat race*

Barrie Day
ISBN # 978-1-59930-015-3

OTHER BOOKS FROM LifeSuccess Publishing

Stop Singing The Blues
*10 Powerful Strategies For
Hitting The High Notes In
Your Life*

Dr. Cynthia Barnett
ISBN # 978-1-59930-022-1

Don't Be A Victim,
Protect Yourself
*Everything Seniors Need To
Know To Avoid Being Taken
Financially*

Jean Ann Dorrell
ISBN # 978-1-59930-024-5

A "Hand Up", not a
"Hand Out"
*The best ways to help others
help themselves*

David Butler
ISBN # 978-1-59930-071-9

Doctor Your Medicine Is
Killing Me!
*One Mans Journey From
Near Death to Health and
Wellness*

Pete Coussa
ISBN # 978-1-59930-047-4

I Believe in Me
*7 Ways for Woman to Step
Ahead in Confidence*

Lisa Gorman
ISBN # 978-1-59930-069-6

The Color of Success
*Why Color Matters in your
Life, your Love, your Lexus*

Mary Ellen Lapp
ISBN # 978-1-59930-078-8

If Not Now, When?
What's Your Dream?

Cindy Nielsen
ISBN # 978-1-59930-073-3

The Skills to Pay the
Bills… and then some!
*How to inspire everyone in
your organisation into high
performance!*

Buki Mosaku
ISBN # 978-1-59930-058-0

OTHER BOOKS FROM LifeSuccess Publishing

P.A.T.C.H.
*5 Strategies to living
your life with purpose.*

Alan W. Goff
ISBN # 978-1-59930-100-6

WE *the new* Me
*Unleash the Creative
Power of Your Mind*

Debbii McKoy
ISBN # 978-159930104--4

The Sweet Smell of Success
Health & Wealth Secrets

James "Tad" Geiger M.D.
ISBN # 978-1-59930-088-7

**Living the Law of
Attraction**
*Real Stories of People
Manifesting Wealth,
Health and Happiness*

Rich German, Andy Wong
& Robin Hoch
ISBN # 978-1-59930-091-7

Wealth Matters
Abundance is Your Birthlight

Chris J. Snook with
Chet Snook
ISBN # 978-1-59930-096-2

The Success Toolbox
For Entrepreneurs

Janis Vos
ISBN # 978-1-59930-005-4

Home Sense
*Dealing with the Trauma
of Renovating your Home*

John Salton
ISBN # 978-1-59930-169-3

**The Girlz Guide to
Building Wealth**
...and men like it too

Maya Galletta, Aaron
Cohen, Polly McCormick,
Mike McCormick
ISBN # 978-1-59930-048-1